Quotes

"I have read the book and am sure it will help many people. It is a book for animal lovers and especially people with pets, or those who have lost pets. It is very Biblical, which means that Christian bookshops will love it. It has certainly raised my awareness of this issue."
Annabel Robson, Commissioning Editor Religious Books, Hodder & Stoughton Publishers, London, England

"You approach a subject which many people do not understand and have strong emotional opinions. I just want you to know your efforts to help pave the future of a better understa. ˙ f the relationship of all living parts of God's Creation is appre ˙ l."
The Rev end A ˙ ewood, FL

"There was always t.. ittle question mark, that is, of course until I read your book. It has been a great blessing to us, now that we know we shall definitely see our beloved pets in Heaven."
Mr. & Mrs. Bill Kerr, Tetford, England

"You are certainly to be commended on your wonderfully revealing and warmth-filled book, "Will I See Fido in Heaven?" I feel that you have performed a much-needed service in your exhaustive research of Biblical references to the immortality of animals."
Dr. William D. Schul, Author, 'Animal Immortality' and 'Life Song', Center for Human Development, Inc., Wichita, KS.

"I am ordering "Will I See Fido in Heaven?" as some of my congregation want to have memorial services for their pets."
The Reverend R. Neil, ME

"This book is an absolute 'must read' and give to prove beyond the shadow of a doubt that have the privilege of spending eternity with ˙ bers."
Sandy Morter, M.Ed., M.S., St. Louis, MO

"As I have to give the sermon at Grace Cathedral in San Francisco on St. Francis' Day when the animals are blessed each year, your book will be very helpful. Thank you so much."
Dr. Jane Goodall, Environmentalist, The Jane Goodall Foundation

"You point out clearly how God wants man to treat animals with respect and use care with all God has made, and if God loves all other creatures, how much more He loves His crowning creation, mankind. The book will be a very effective witness to those who are animal lovers, but who have not considered their own relationship with God."
Pastor Tom Smith, Grace Church, St. Louis, MO.

"I wish to thank you for your beautifully written book. Many years ago, I was concerned about the immortality of animals. I knew that an All Loving Merciful GOD would not have created these innocent creatures only to have them suffer and die as a finality. I found most of those Scriptures that you brought out in your book. I would never be able to understand how anyone who reads your book could ever doubt the immortality of animals.
R. Johnson, West Covina, CA

"I'll always treasure this book, as it has given me a deeper understanding of the relationship between God, man and animals. The book contains a wealth of material which gives me peace and comfort. I thank you again for all you did to make the loss of my little Tiffany easier to accept."
Esther LaRocque, Plainview, MN

"I love your book!"
Jack Hanna, Director, The Columbus Zoo, Columbus, OH

This book answers the question that so many people ask about God's relationship with the animals. It brings out the Bible's teaching for us.
Reverend Martin Down, Vicar, Norfolk England

I am the founder of an organization that helps humans and animals during times of crisis involving the pet. We ultimately strive to give love, encouragement, faith, peace and understanding to those who mourn the loss of their beloved animals. "Will I See Fido in Heaven?" is a wonderful source of knowledge and comfort and should be made available to everyone who is receptive.
Bruce Redmond Griswold, Atlanta, GA

Will I See Fido in Heaven?

Scripturally Revealing God's
Eternal Plan for His Lesser Creatures.

Mary Buddemeyer-Porter

Eden Publications
Manchester, Missouri
www.creaturesinheaven.com

Eden Publications Press Edition, 2000

First Published 1995
First Revised Printing 2000

The following Bibles and resource materials were used for *Will I See Fido in Heaven?*
New Catholic Edition of the Holy Bible (1948)
King James Version (KJV)
The New Jerusalem Version (NJB)
The Living Bible (TLB)
New International Version (NIV)
Revised Standard Version (RSV)
New American Bible (NAB)
The Amplified Bible (AMP)
The Good News Bible (TEV)
Douay Rheims Version (1899)
The Holy Scriptures (1917)
World's Bible Dictionary (1990)
Matthew Henry's Commentary (1961)
The NIV Matthew Henry Commentary (1992)
The Dead Sea Scrolls Uncovered (1992)

ISBN 1-56043-553-4

Cover design by Lisa Ducioame
Author's portrait by Roman Buddemeyer

For Worldwide Distribution
Printed in the United States of America

Acknowledgments

I wish to thank the following people for their prayers and assistance in making *Will I See Fido in Heaven?* possible:

My husband, Ron, who has tolerated and nurtured all the stray and helpless dogs I have brought into our home and shared my love with. Mr. and Mrs. James Jensen, Marilyn Jones, Mac Allen Edwards, Vi Massa, Michael Magliari, Joe and Jan Jeziorski, Randy Manley, Lana Richard, and Bill and Lynn Seebold for sharing their animal stories. Eden, Lisa, Brittany, Roman and Heidi Buddemeyer, Jamie and Amanda Fritz, Paula Baker, Wayne Porter and Doreen, and Sandy Morter for their help and encouragement. All the pastors, especially Pastor Tom Smith, for their wonderful support, comments, and advice. Sharon Turner and Sandra and Perry Sneed for the research of Bible verses, commentary, and Scripture additions. A very special thanks goes to Eric and Debbie Freesmeier for their prayers of encouragement. Karla Harris and Lisa Ducioame for their initial editing. Heartfelt thanks goes to Gladys Seitter for her resource searches, and St. Louis Concordia Seminary/Library Reference Department for their assistance.

I pray that all those who have worked so diligently on this book be abundantly blessed. Lloyd Heidebrand, whose marvelous editorial transformation of the manuscript, led by the Holy Spirit, wonderfully brought to life God's message. Eva Ball and Reggie Powell, the liaisons at Destiny Image, through their prayers and servitude as Christians, pulled together all concerns of the various personalities to keep God the focus of the book.

Thanks to Sheila Boyd for her perfection in copy editing and Scripture verification. Her contributions have been invaluable to all who have worked so hard to bring *Will I See Fido in Heaven?* to you. I also want to extend my sincere thanks to Jeanette Martin. Through God's guidance she has perfected the editorial transformation of commentary and Scripture.

Special thanks to Roger Fritz for his wonderful foreword and commentary throughout the book. Roger's commitment and direction gave the focus necessary to bring *Will I See Fido in Heaven?* to print.

Most of all, I thank God for directing me to write on earth what He has prepared for us in Heaven.

Contents

About the Book

Many Christians do not believe that animals go to Heaven. I have to admit that for more than 40 years, I was one of them. But I had always hoped that animals would be in Heaven and I asked God to reveal to me if they would or would not be there.

One day in 1988, as I was reading the Book of Romans, I came to chapter 8, verses 18 through 23, in The Living Bible. In those verses I found new meaning concerning animals and God's eternal promise to them. Until that day I had seen only His promise of eternal life for His children. Not being sure I had fully understood the meaning of the verses, I read them in the King James Version. My understanding of the meaning of that Scripture remained the same. Then I thought, *If animals truly are found in Heaven, then the Book of Genesis should give some more indication of God's plan for all His creatures from the beginning of creation.* To my wondrous surprise, I found that God included the animals in His covenant with Noah. In fact, each of the seven times He spoke of His covenant with Noah, He also included the animals.

By then my confidence of seeing my pets in Heaven was growing stronger. I thought that if all the animals will be in Heaven, then surely the apostle John, in his vision of Heaven and the eternal promise God has given us, will also indicate that animals will be in Heaven. Sure enough, in Revelation

5:8-13 all creatures recognize Jesus as the Savior of the world and praise God right along with redeemed men.

From that point on, I specifically asked for guidance through the Holy Spirit to indicate three places in the Bible concerning the following: Do animals have a soul and spirit? Are they sinful or sinless? Do animals have wisdom and insight? I found the answers to each question restated in many books of the Bible, both in the Old and New Testaments. An added surprise was Scripture stating that animals praise and recognize God as their Creator and Provider. Much more became evident as I researched the Scriptures concerning animals. I also asked God for a born-again, Spirit-filled person to direct me and add to the writing of the book. God provided me with a wonderful Christian, Roger Fritz.

All my life I have hurt when I lost an animal. Yet, growing up on a farm, I did not feel badly when other animals were used as meat. We realize that all creatures must physically die. However, as we look back to the Book of Genesis before man fell into sin, none of God's creatures ate each other. Man brought physical death to all creation when he sinned. When you realize that life does not end at physical death, the pain of losing an animal is not so bad.

Will I See Fido in Heaven? is from God and of God, and its truth will bring many to God. I am grateful that I am allowed to be a vessel through which God brings the good news about the creatures He has made and will have throughout eternity. And, in doing so, I will be able to share the sacrifice Christ made for each of us. It is the prayer of both Roger and me that you too will find joy and peace about your eternal destination.

Mary Buddemeyer-Porter

Foreword

When Mary first asked me to work with her on this project, I was admittedly reluctant and a little skeptical. Her topic, "Do animals go to Heaven?" was not a fervent issue for me. It wasn't that I necessarily disagreed with Mary's beliefs; it was just that I had never seriously considered the subject before.

Anyone who knows Mary has felt the tenacity of her Spirit-filled enthusiasm. Out of respect for her devotion to the project and her sincerity as a Christian, I felt led to help her. I'm thankful that I did.

This book is dedicated to animal lovers and it fulfills its mission delightfully by demonstrating God's eternal plan for all of creation. References to Scripture and real-life stories are skillfully combined to create a thought-provoking vision of the relationship between God, man, and animals.

We ask you to join in this journey and read the book with an open mind and an open heart. You will not only increase your appreciation of the animal kingdom, you also will find clarity concerning fundamental spiritual truths. The distinction between spirit, soul, and body; the impact of guilt, fear, and anger; and the role of compassion, sacrifice, and forgiveness are applied to both animals and man. These principles and supporting Scriptures provide the underlying structure for the book.

More importantly, receive the faith to look forward with assurance that what God reveals through His Word will come to pass.

Roger Fritz

Preface

Do animals have a soul? Do animals have a spirit? Do animals sin? Do animals need forgiveness? What does Scripture say about God's plan for His creatures?

The answers may surprise you. We invite you to take a scriptural journey from the Garden of Eden to the Second Coming of Christ and learn about God's plan for us and for the animals.

Introduction

Although I am a Protestant, God miraculously made the books of the Apocrypha from the Catholic Bible available to me. I did not understand why I had the Catholic Bible until after I started reading some of the books not found in the Protestant Bible. Passages from two of the Apocrypha books, Ecclesiasticus (or the Book of Sirach) and Wisdom, wonderfully pull together many of the Scriptures found in various translations of the Protestant Bible. They make clear the final outcome of good and evil for man and the animals. Passages from these books not only support the Protestant Bible, but also add depth to it. They make the message easier to understand, and add credence concerning the eternal destination of both man and animals.

I do believe the Word of God is the truth. God started this project when He put a love for His creation in my heart. *Will I See Fido in Heaven?* was written to honor God, the wonders of His creation, and the eternal love He has for all He created. The Bible says: "Being confident of this very thing, that he which hath begun a good work in you will perform *it* until the day of Jesus Christ:" (Philippians 1:6 KJV).

The Old Testament tells us that man needed sacrificial animals to cover sin. Why animals? The Bible tells us that, unlike man, the lesser creatures are innocent.

Animals did not need an intercessor; they were, and are, incapable of sin. Romans 8:20 says the animals were put under vanity (worthlessness, false pride), which ends in physical death, because of the sins of man. It is not due to their sins.

Chapter I

Animals and Eternal Life

And God saw every thing that he had made, and, behold, it was *very good* (Genesis 1:31a KJV).

My Search for an Answer

As I stop to think about the beauty of this world, I realize that it is not the material things that bring us joy, peace, love, and purpose. Rather, it is God and His creations—our families, our pets, the trees, and flowers—therefore, we could say it is nature that brings us fulfillment. Humans are often awestruck with God's creation and how everything works together in perfect rhythm. Animals, in particular, entertain and amaze us. As pets, they quickly capture our hearts and become a precious part of our lives. Can we really imagine Heaven without them?

There was a time in my life when I questioned whether God existed. I was not looking forward to an eternal life because I could not imagine living without the animals I cherished. At that time, I did not understand what the Scriptures reveal about the lesser animals and their eternal union with God. Then, one cool November day in 1965, Jesus came into my life and I became a different person. Oh, I had gone to church all my life, but I had never, until that day in November, received Jesus as my Lord and Savior. That day I knew I was forgiven for my sins, and the Holy Spirit came to live inside me. I was truly a new creature in Christ. My rebirth was not unlike that of other Christians who have found Christ. The Bible says: "Therefore if any man *be* in Christ, *he is* a new creature: old things are passed away; behold, all things are become new" (II Corinthians 5:17 KJV). As a new creation filled with God's Holy and revealing Spirit, I was beginning to understand things beyond the physical world. The Scriptures started to become clear to me.

I now know that in this life, both the joy and the suffering which people and animals encounter is simply part of the preparation for the fulfillment we all will receive in the future. The temporary hunger we experience now simply foreshadows an abundance of nourishment in Heaven that is beyond our comprehension. The apostle Paul says: "For I reckon that the sufferings of this present time *are* not worthy *to be compared* with the glory which shall be revealed in us" (Romans 8:18 KJV).

I now realize that the animals I have loved will indeed be with me in Heaven. Romans 8:19 (KJV) says that the lesser creatures await Christ's return to redeem the sons of God so they, too, will be released from physical death to eternal life.

The Book of Revelation looks into the future when all creatures will recognize Jesus (the Lamb of God), the King of kings. Every creature in Heaven, on the earth, under the earth, and in the sea will praise Him. They will all recognize Jesus. The Book of Revelation says:

> *And every creature which is in heaven, and on the earth, and under the earth, and such as are in the sea, and all that are in them, heard I saying, Blessing, and honour, and glory, and power, be unto him that sitteth upon the throne, and unto the Lamb for ever and ever* (Revelation 5:13 KJV).

The Impact of Sin

The Scriptures say that animals are not of themselves sinners, but are subject to the results of sin—not of their own accord, but because of man's sins. Because of man, they are contaminated and have become corrupted. The King James Version of the Bible uses the word *vanity* to mean emptiness, or worthlessness. Vanity was man's first sin. Vanity affected man to the point that he thought he could be his own god. Thus man sinned and separated himself spiritually from God. In doing this, he brought death to all physically breathing life forms. Like all living things, the animals became worthless. As stated in Genesis 2:17–3:19,22-23 of the King James Version of the Bible, all life had to be destroyed to end sin's eternal control over the world. Now, all living things are subject to destruction: "For the creature was made subject to vanity, not willingly, but by reason of him who hath subjected *the same* in hope" (Romans 8:20 KJV).

God subjected animals to death just as He did man. However, in doing so, God also gave them hope for the future when Christ will rescue them from their physical bondage. Paul wrote in the Book of Romans: "Because the creature itself also shall be delivered from the bondage of corruption into the glorious liberty of the children of God. For we know that the whole creation groaneth and travaileth in pain together until now" (Romans 8:21-22 KJV).

As stated in *The NIV Matthew Henry Commentary*: "The end and purpose of God's giving renewing grace, *That we might be a kind of firstfruits of all he created.* Christ is the firstfruits of Christians, Christians are the firstfruits of creation."[1] The apostle James wrote that the sons/children of God are the kind of firstfruits of God's creation, of all His creatures (see James 1:18 KJV). This gives us insight into the distinction, or separation, between God's creatures. According to Romans 8:23 (AMP), animals must await the redemption of the firstfruits before they, too, can be redeemed:

> *And not only the creation, but we ourselves too, who have* and *enjoy the firstfruits of the (Holy) Spirit—a foretaste of the blissful things to come—groan inwardly as we wait for the redemption of our bodies [from sensuality and the grave,*

which will reveal] our adoption (our manifestation as God's sons) (Romans 8:23 AMP).

The angels, God's third set of creatures, do not wait for the renewal of their bodies (except for demon angels who are cast into the abyss with Satan). Therefore, the word *creature*, as used in Romans 8:21, must refer to only animals and not to man or angels. James says: "Of his own will begat he us with the word of truth, that we should be a kind of firstfruits of his creatures" (James 1:18 KJV). Although both man and animals go to Heaven, man dominates. According to the Scriptures, man, as firstfruits, will one day inherit the Kingdom as joint heirs with Christ.

Richard Bauckham, Professor of New Testament Studies at St. Mary's College, University of St. Andrews, and a writer, elaborates on man's separation from nature. He explains that this separation sometimes results in violence. He is quoted as saying in Leon Morris' book, *The Cross of Jesus*:

> "Since humanity is the dominant species on earth, human sin is bound to have very widespread effects on nature as a whole. The fall disturbed humanity's harmonious relationship with nature, alienating us from nature, so that we now experience nature as hostile, and introducing elements of struggle and violence into our relationship with nature" (see Genesis 3:15; 17-19; 9:2 KJV).[2]

> *And I will put enmity between thee and the woman, and between thy seed and her seed; it shall bruise thy head, and thou shalt bruise his heel* (Genesis 3:15 KJV).

> *And unto Adam he said, Because thou hast hearkened unto the voice of thy wife, and hast eaten of the tree, of which I commanded thee, saying, Thou shalt not eat of it: cursed is the ground for thy sake; in sorrow shalt thou eat of it all the days of thy life; Thorns also and thistles shall it bring forth to thee; and thou shalt eat the herb of the field; In the sweat of thy face shalt thou eat bread, till thou return unto the*

ground; for out of it wast thou taken: for dust thou art, *and unto dust shalt thou return* (Genesis 3:17-19 KJV).

And the fear of you and the dread of you shall be upon every beast of the earth, and upon every fowl of the air, upon all that moveth upon *the earth, and upon all the fishes of the sea; into your hand are they delivered* (Genesis 9:2 KJV).

Because we misuse nature, nature suffers and awaits our full redemption.

Futility and Frustration

The Amplified Bible gives a clear picture of how the animals await Jesus' return along with Christians. It says:

For (even the whole) creation (all nature) waits expectantly and *longs earnestly for God's sons to be made known—waits for the revealing, the disclosing of their sonship. For the creation (nature) was subjected to frailty—to futility, condemned to frustration—not because of some intentional fault on its part, but by the will of Him Who so subjected it. [Yet] with the hope* (Romans 8:19-20 AMP; see Ecclesiastes 1:2).

That nature (creation) itself will be set free from its bondage to decay and *corruption [and gain an entrance] into the glorious freedom of God's children. We know that the whole creation (of irrational creatures) has been moaning together in the pains of labor until now* (Romans 8:21-22 AMP; see Jeremiah 12:4,11).

The Scriptures refer to the futility and frustration that both animals and man incur. What does futility imply? It means uselessness; being incapable of producing any results; worthlessness. According to the Scriptures, all God's creatures are subjected to futility. Why do people suffer? Why do the animals and creation suffer? All suffer because of the sins of man. Before sin entered the world, life was not empty or futile. Neither man nor animals had frustration. Life for both would go on endlessly. But man sinned. The Book of

Romans says: "Because that, when they knew God, they glorified *him* not as God, neither were thankful; but became vain in their imaginations, and their foolish heart was darkened" (Romans 1:21 KJV).

In the third chapter of Leon Morris' book, *The Cross of Jesus,* he speaks of the meaning of creature and the answer to futility in creation in reference to Romans 8:19-23. Morris says:

> "Some scholars see a reference to mankind, possibly especially to unregenerate mankind, in these words. But it is hard to believe that this was Paul's meaning. He cannot be referring to the regenerate, for he differentiates the saved from 'the whole creation'. Nor can he mean the unregenerate, for he does not regard them as being brought into the liberty of the glory of the sons of God. It is unlikely that the words refer to good angels, for they were not subjected to the futility of which Paul writes, or to evil angels, for they are not looking forward to the revelation of the sons of God. Paul is surely referring to the whole creation below the personal level; he is speaking of animals and birds and trees and flowers."[3]

Now all the creatures of the world experience frustration. Can this frustration be relieved with hope? Hope in what? The Book of Romans says:

> *And not only they, but ourselves also, which have the first fruits of the Spirit, even we ourselves groan within ourselves, waiting for the adoption, to wit, the redemption of our body. For we are saved by hope: but hope that is seen is not hope: for what a man seeth, why doth he yet hope for?* (Romans 8:23-24 KJV).

Yes, our hope and the hope of creation, including the animals, is in Jesus Christ. *Matthew Henry's Commentary* (on Romans 8:19-22) explains the plight of the creatures' earthly lives and their longing for the future. Jesus sacrificed His life on the cross so all God's creatures could have eternal life. When they physically die, all God's lesser creatures will be liberated from this world of corruption for the new Heaven and new earth, and will be free from the frustration and futility of this life.

The following is from *Matthew Henry's Commentary* on Romans 8:19-22:

"That must needs be a great, a transcendent glory, which all the creatures are so earnestly expecting and longing for. By the *creature* here we understand the whole frame of nature, the whole creation. The sense of the apostle in these four verses we may take in the following observations: (1) There is a present vanity to which the creature, by reason of the sin of man, is made subject, v. 20. When man sinned, the ground was cursed for man's sake, and with it all the creatures. *Under the bondage of corruption,* v. 21. The creation is sullied and stained, much of the beauty of the world gone. And it is not the least part of their bondage that they are used, or abused rather, by men as instruments of sin. And this *not willingly,* not of their own choice. All the creatures desire their own perfection. When they are made instruments of sin it is not willingly. They are thus captivated, not for any sin of their own, but for man's sin: *By reason of him who hath subjected the same.* And this yoke (poor creatures) they bear in hope that it will not be so always. We have reason to pity the poor creatures that for our sin have become subject to vanity. (2) The creatures *groan and travail in pain* together under this vanity and corruption, v. 22. Sin is a burden to the whole creation. There is a general outcry of the whole creation against the sin of man. (3) The creature shall be *delivered from this bondage into the glorious liberty of the children of God* (v. 21)—they shall no more be subject to

vanity and corruption. This lower world shall be renewed: when there will be new heavens there will be a
new earth. (4) The creature doth therefore earnestly
expect the *manifestation of the children of God*, v. 19.
Now the saints are God's hidden ones, the wheat
seems lost in a heap of chaff; but then they shall be
manifested. The children of God shall appear in their
own colours. And this redemption of the creature is
reserved till then. This the whole creation longs for;
and it may serve as a reason why now a good man
should be merciful to his beast."[4]

Therefore, according to Matthew Henry, the frustration
and imperfections caused by sin continue to affect all of nature. The frustration put on all creation has caused endless
suffering and pain, however, to many of God's animals.
There are people who try to right the wrongs put on animals
due to man's lack of concern and irresponsibility. For instance, a family I know felt great compassion for an injured,
neglected dog that lived near their home. Because of their
love, a dog named Ricky was able to live a long, happy life
with people who really cared about him. Ricky's story illustrates the frustration and futility inflicted on animals because of man's sins. I would like to share his story with you.

A Dog Named Ricky

*Our accountant, Vi Massa, told me about a dog named
Ricky her family adopted when she was 11. Vi's family lived
near a wealthy estate in St. Louis. The family living on the estate kept large Great Dane guard dogs. One day the chauffeur
working on the estate ran over the back leg of one of the dogs.
The chauffeur, knowing that the wealthy family would not
want to care for the injured dog, finally asked Vi's family if they
would take care of it. Since Vi and her family loved animals,
they agreed to care for the dog, whose name was Ricky.*

*Because Ricky's leg had been left unattended for some time,
it became badly infected. A local veterinarian said he could get*

rid of the infection but there were splinters of bone in the leg. These splinters would need to be removed every few weeks as they worked their way to the surface of the skin. He said Ricky would probably never be able to walk on his hind leg. In short, there would be many trips to the animal hospital to remove the painful splinters. This meant several unpleasant operations for Ricky. Vi's family fell in love with Ricky, though, and decided to keep him after being told the wealthy family did not want a crippled dog.

In those days, there weren't many people living in Vi's area, and Ricky was allowed to roam their large yard. One day Vi's mother received a call from the veterinarian who said Ricky had appeared at the animal hospital. He scratched on the front door and came right in when the vet opened it. Ricky had apparently sought out the vet so he could remove some of the painful splinters from the hind leg. The good doctor operated and then called Vi's family to come and take him home. The family was shocked to find that Ricky had made his way to the veterinarian all by himself. Since Ricky could not walk on his back leg, it seemed almost impossible that he had limped there on his own. But apparently Ricky had been more observant on that first trip than they realized. Vi's family picked up Ricky and brought him home again. But, a few weeks later, Ricky again appeared on his own at the hospital. He needed another operation. Again the vet called Vi's family when he had finished removing some more bone splinters from Ricky's leg. This scenario was repeated several times. Although Ricky could never use his injured leg, he made it to the vet's every time he was in pain and needed another operation. The vet was so amazed with Ricky that he never charged Vi's family for his services.

Scripture reveals that Ricky will not be crippled in Heaven. The Epistle of Paul the Apostle to the Philippians says: "Who shall change our vile body, that it may be fashioned like unto his glorious body, according to the working

whereby he is able even to subdue all things unto himself"
(Philippians 3:21 KJV). Ricky's body will be made perfect
just as the bodies of people with physical and mental handi-
caps will be. God will change animals' corruptible bodies
into new, perfect bodies just as He will with us.

In God's new Heaven and earth, all bodies will be turned
into perfect, everlasting bodies. Let's read First Corinthians
15:35-43 in The Living Bible. It compares the perfecting of
the body to a seed buried, then brought back to life in its glorious new perfection. It says:

> *But someone may ask, "How will the dead be brought back
> to life again? What kind of bodies will they have?" What a
> foolish question! You will find the answer in your own gar-
> den! When you put a seed into the ground it doesn't grow
> into a plant unless it "dies" first. And when the green shoot
> comes up out of the seed, it is very different from the seed you
> first planted. For all you put into the ground is a dry little
> seed of wheat, or whatever it is you are planting, then God
> gives it a beautiful new body—just the kind he wants it to
> have; a different kind of plant grows from each kind of seed.
> And just as there are different kinds of seeds and plants, so
> also there are different kinds of flesh. Humans, animals,
> fish, and birds are all different. The angels in heaven have
> bodies far different from ours, and the beauty and the glory
> of their bodies is different from the beauty and the glory of
> ours. The sun has one kind of glory while the moon and
> stars have another kind. And the stars differ from each other
> in their beauty and brightness. In the same way, our earthly
> bodies which die and decay are different from the bodies we
> shall have when we come back to life again, for they will
> never die. The bodies we have now embarrass us for they be-
> come sick and die; but they will be full of glory when we
> come back to life again. Yes, they are weak, dying bodies
> now, but when we live again they will be full of strength*
> (I Corinthians 15:35-43 TLB).

Seventeenth-century theologian John Wesley (1703-91), founder of the Methodist Church, stated in his sermon entitled "The General Deliverance":

"But will 'the creature,' will even the brute creature, always remain in this deplorable condition? God forbid that we should affirm this; yea, or even entertain such a thought! While 'the whole creation groaneth together,' (whether men attend or not,) their groans are not dispersed in idle air, but enter into the ears of Him that made them. While his creatures 'travail together in pain,' he knoweth all their pain, and is bringing them nearer and nearer to the birth, which shall be accomplished in its season. He seeth 'the earnest expectation' wherewith the whole animated creation 'waiteth for' that final 'manifestation of the sons of God;' in which 'they themselves also shall be delivered' (not by annihilation; annihilation is not deliverance) 'from the' present 'bondage of corruption, into' a measure of 'the glorious liberty of the children of God.'

"A general view of this is given us in the twenty-first chapter of the Revelation. When He that 'sitteth on the great white throne' hath pronounced, 'Behold, I make all things new;' when the word is fulfilled, 'The tabernacle of God is with men, and they shall be his people, and God himself shall be with them, and be their God;'—then the following blessing shall take place (not only on the children of men; there is no such restriction in the text; but) on every creature according to its capacity: 'God shall wipe away all tears from their eyes. And there shall be no more death, neither sorrow, nor crying, neither shall there be any more pain: for the former things are passed away.' "[5]

The following story, "A Child Blessed," gives great insight into the understanding of a dimension of the world

that we, from a human perspective, cannot recognize. Jesus
was able to give comfort to children and hope for the future
for all the creatures they loved. The story is from the book
Jesus Loved Them by Omar Garrison, and is now out of print.
The story is said to be told by the Beloved Apostle John
while he was with Jesus during our Savior's earthly ministry.
I found the story as I was reading some of my father's old
Christian books, and *Reader's Digest* published it in 1958. I
wish to thank both the author and the publishers for uncov-
ering this wonderful story about Jesus, the little boy, and his
dog.

A Child Blessed

*Jesus loved little children because in the purity of their
hearts and the innocence of their enchanted world, they often
understood Him better than did His gruff, mature disciples. So
He never turned them away, whether their mothers had
brought them to be blessed, or to be cured of some illness.*

*There is a beautiful story, unsupported by Scripture, told of
how Jesus one day comforted a child whose dog had died. This
story was told by John, who has been named the Beloved Disci-
ple, unto peoples of the North countries:*

*John said: "I remember once He found a small boy weeping
for his dog that lay dead beside him. And Jesus lifted up the
child and told him: 'Animals live a different way from men and
they see what few men see on earth. And often he befriendeth
man, as thy furry friend lingereth now to draw thy vision from
the earth that ye may see beyond this world in which men also
die.'*

*"Jesus lifted the small hand and placed within its palm a
token—a small shell that He had found on the shore that morning, and had carried in His tunic. He explained that the small
creature who had once lived within this house had left it.*

*" 'Now pause a moment, watch the shell and listen,' He told
the child. And the child gave rapt attention to the little shell,
and listened to the story of the sea, learning how a small shell
could house a living creature who might depart, and yet not die.*

And that it is God's plan that everything in the experience of boys and men must change." [6]

Since he was one of the original disciples of Jesus, John knew Jesus well. Because of this, John had insight into what was ahead for all of God's creatures, including the animals.

More Than Just Prey

According to George Mac Donald in his book, *The Hope of the Gospel*, some Christians believe that God made many of the lower creatures merely for prey; that He created (and is still creating) an endless succession of animals to reap little or no good other than to contribute to the continuation of life. To believe in this doctrine, he feels, is to believe in a God who, so far as one portion of His creation is concerned, is a demon. The concept of a demon creator in itself is not an absurdity; but if such a creator was possible, he would not be God, but would be found and destroyed by the real God.[7]

Matthew says: "Are not two sparrows sold for a farthing? and one of them shall not fall on the ground without your Father" (Matthew 10:29 KJV). Mac Donald goes on to say, "If His presence be no good to the sparrow, are you very sure what good it will be to you when your hour comes? Why is God there, if His presence is not of any good to the sparrow? If the Father will raise His children, why should He not also raise those that He has taught His little ones to love? Love is the one bond of the universe, the heart of God, the life of His children. If animals can be loved, they are lovable; if they can love, they are yet more plainly lovable. Since love is eternal, how then should its object perish?"

George Mac Donald goes on to state: "When you say then that for the children of God there is no more death, remember that the deliverance of the creature is from the bondage of corruption into the glorious liberty of the children of God." All creatures, except for the angels, are waiting for their earthly physical bodies to be renewed into glorious new bodies without any more pain and physical death.

The Dead Sea Scrolls are ancient manuscripts from Palestine placed in caves almost 2,000 years ago near the northwestern shore of the Dead Sea. They were found by a shepherd boy in 1947. Considered to be the greatest discovery of modern time, the scrolls include all the books of the Old Testament except Esther and are the oldest known manuscripts of any books of the Bible.

"The Dead Sea Scrolls Uncovered" by Robert Eisenman and Michael Wise includes the first translation and interpretation of 50 key documents withheld for over 35 years. Within the text was discovered more evidence of the eternal life of the lesser creatures. The following manuscripts from the Dead Sea Scrolls are consistent with Romans 8:23, which speaks of the redemption (renewing) of the physical body, and Revelation 5:13, which speaks of the praise of all creation to God and the Lamb forever and ever.

The Splendour of the Spirits

Manuscript B Fragment 1 *(9) and all the servants of Ho{liness...} (10) in the Perfection of th{eir} works... (11) in {their} wond{rous} Temples...(12) {a}ll {their] servant[s ...} (13) Your Holiness in the habitat{ion of...}* **Fragment 2** *(1)...them, and they shall bless Your Holy Name with blessing{s}...(2) and they shall bless} You, all creatures of flesh in unison, whom {You} have creat{ed...(3) be}asts and birds and reptiles and the fish of the seas, and all...(4) {Y}ou have created them all anew...* **Fragment 3** *(13)... The Holy Spirit {sett}led upon His Messiah...*

The Messianic and Visionary Recitals

This manuscript appears to be Ezekiel's vision of the new heaven.

(9) Now behold, a city will be built for the Name of the Great One, {the Eternal Lord}...{And no} (10) evil shall be committed in the presence of the Great One, {the Eternal Lord...(11) Then the Great One, the Eternal Lord, will remember His creation {for the purpose of Good}... {Blessing and honor and praise} (12) {be to} the Great One, the Eternal Lord.

Chapter II

Body, Soul, Spirit—
Animals and Man

For the word of God is quick, and powerful, and sharper than any twoedged sword, piercing even to the dividing asunder of soul and spirit... (Hebrews 4:12 KJV).

Who doesn't know that the Lord does things like that? Ask the dumbest beast—he knows that it is so; ask the birds—they will tell you; or let the earth teach you, or the fish of the sea. For the soul of every living thing is in the hand of God, and the breath of all mankind (Job 12:7-10 TLB).

The Order of Creation

In the beginning, God created the angels. Then He made the heavens, the earth, and the water. He separated the light from the darkness; He spoke and the earth brought forth vegetation; and God said it was good. Next, God made the animals. He blessed them and told them to multiply. God said they, too, were good.

Next, God made man and formed him in His own image. God blessed Adam and Eve and told them to multiply on the earth. God gave man dominion over the animals.

All life, including the plants, had a bodily form. Originally, all had physical properties that were designed to live forever. On a scientific level, every cell in the body recreates itself within an 11-year cycle; thus, the physical body is actually designed for continual recreation. This changed, however, when sin entered the soul of man.

In this chapter, we will discuss the body, soul, and spirit of the animals. Sometimes, the understanding of distinguishing the soul from the spirit is difficult to grasp. By observing nature, and comparing various aspects of animals to man, many scientists and biblical scholars believe that animals have a soul and spirit; yet oftentimes theologians are naive of the basic biblical foundation substantiating the soul and spirit of all God's creatures. Thus many of us have had a difficult time believing it. With careful study of the Bible, however, we can see that the Scriptures say both animals and man are made in the same way. God gives life and breath to every creature.

God made both man and animals out of the earth, out of the material He had already created. Physically, both man and animals were made of the same material—the dust of the earth. From dust all physical bodies came and to dust will all physical bodies return, as stated in Genesis 3:19, Job 40:15, and Ecclesiastes 3:20. "In the sweat of thy face shalt thou eat bread, till thou return unto the ground; for out of it wast thou taken: for dust thou *art*, and unto dust shalt thou return" (Genesis 3:19 KJV). "Behold now behemoth, which I made with thee; he eateth grass as an ox" (Job 40:15 KJV). "All go unto one place; all are of the dust, and all turn to dust again" (Ecclesiastes 3:20 KJV).

There is a spiritual death, which means spiritual separation from God. There is also a physical death. Upon physical death the spirit and soul continue to live on, but not in the physical body.

Defining Body, Soul, and Spirit

Let us define body, soul, and spirit according to the Holy Bible and the *World's Bible Dictionary*:

Body

A body is a mortal, earthly, physical being. It is made of flesh, bones, blood, etc., and is distinct from the soul and spirit. The body is living only when the soul and spirit remain in the physical body. (See Micah 6:7 KJV; Matthew 10:28 KJV; Romans 7:23-25 KJV.) The body represents the living man, or animals, in a physical state. The body must be physically fed to grow, develop, and sustain an earthly existence.

Soul

In the Old Testament, the soul means "being." The soul is the living being of a person or an animal. The soul can be part of, or apart from, the physical body. Man is of a higher order than the animals (the soul is called *nephesh* in Hebrew). The soul is the psyche, the mind, the emotions, the self-image—the psychological being apart from the spiritual being. The soul must be mentally fed to grow. Both the lesser animals and man have a soul. The King James Authorized Version, revised and edited by W.C. Sanderson, indicates in a footnote that "soul" or "living soul" are alternative translations for "life."[8] A few places in the Bible have kept the original translation; Numbers 31:28 is one of them.

Dr. E.D. Buckner, M.D., wrote *The Immortality of Animals* in 1903. His message and research through Scripture and science, being himself a doctor of medicine and a scholar of research on theologians and theology, is quite profound. He makes two important points. First, Dr. Buckner says, "I accept the Bible as a Divine Revelation, and take the Mosaic description of creation as a basis of my work." He identified many well-known theologians who recognize the immortality of animals.

There is a law in physics that says nothing is lost, and so we reason. All potential forces and substances in nature are indestructible and eternal. Matter and soul (or mind) are the only constituent elements in the universe, and they both exist in man and the lower animals alike.

Second, Dr. Buckner says this:

"Here, for the first and only time, the particular manner of how life was imparted was given in the case of Adam. Genesis 2:7 says, 'God breathed into his nostrils the breath of life; and man became a living soul.' As to what methods were used to impart life to the other animals and to Eve we are not informed. No animal could live without the breath of life, and as the divine writer said nothing about the manner of its being imparted, it must be assumed that God breathed into the animals and the woman, the breath of life and they became living souls. Any other assumption would be illogical. In reference to the flood, Genesis 7:21,22 says: 'All flesh died that moved upon the earth, both of fowl, and of cattle, and of beasts, and of every creeping thing, and every man, all *in whose nostrils* was the breath of life.' It is acknowledged by all the best Greek and Hebrew scholars today that, in every passage of Scripture where the Hebrew word *nephesh* or the Greek word *psyche* is used, it should be translated soul, and when *nephesh chayah* is used it should be translated living soul. This is admitted by the marginal reading found in many old English Bibles. In Genesis 2:7 when God speaks of Adam, the translation is correct, as it reads in the Hebrew, *nephesh chayah*, which translated into English means a living soul; but there are nine more passages in Genesis where the same Hebrew words are used, but as they refer to lower animals the true meaning has been perverted by the English translation. We read: 'God said, Let the waters bring forth abundantly the moving creature that hath a *living soul*.' The Hebrew text reads *nephesh*, soul, and *chayah*, living and the English version has it 'life,' but on the margin of many Bibles 'living soul.' Again we read, 'And God created great whales and every *living soul.*' Hebrew, *nephesh chayah*, the English version, 'living creature.' Again we read, 'And God said, Let the earth bring forth the *living soul* after its kind, cattle and creeping things and beasts of the earth,' yet the English version has it 'living creature,' and 'To every beast of the earth and to every fowl of the air and to everything that creepeth upon the earth wherein there is a *living soul.*' "[9]

Dr. Buckner examined a large number of Bibles and stopped when he found 100 giving the words *living soul* in the margin where the word *life* is used in the text of the English version. If God, in His revealed Word, had intended to convey the idea that man was created immortal and animals were not, He certainly would not have made a plain statement that all were created alike.

And levy a tribute unto the Lord of the men of war which went out to battle: one soul of five hundred, both of the persons, and of the beeves, and of the asses, and of the sheep (Numbers 31:28 KJV).

The soul perceives, thinks, feels, and makes decisions and choices. In man, the soul can also sin. God gave man the choice to choose sin or righteousness, to worship himself or God.

The lesser animals were not given this choice. God put them under the protection and dominion of man. This eventually was harmful for creation because man's heart/soul is selfish. Man is often self-centered and puts himself above others. The Bible says: "The heart is the most deceitful thing there is, and desperately wicked. No one can really know how bad it is!" (Jeremiah 17:9 TLB).

Although animals die physically because of the sins of man, their souls have not been contaminated due to their own sins. When an animal kills, it is for survival, since man's original sin altered all of nature. Animals forgive and are at

peace with the world. They are by nature mentally and physically healthy. When allowed to live free, animals do not exhibit the emotional and physiological trauma as they do
when they are forced to exist in small, closed-in areas.
Though man's reasoning abilities, communication skills, and
emotional complexities are much greater than those of the
lesser animals, science is discovering that animals, such as
dogs, dolphins, and baboons, also have the ability to make
decisions. Scientists now understand that animals can communicate with people, especially with handicapped people.
The lesser animals also deal with feelings and forgiveness.
Some animals, because of constant abuse, become defensive
and exhibit fear. Yet, even abused animals can learn to trust
again when they are treated with love and respect.

Each person has a unique personality, psyche, or soul.
We are recognized for our talents and mental abilities.
These aspects make up our soul. Each animal also has a soul
that reveals something about it. For instance, each of our
dogs has a unique personality. One dog loves to play in
water and snow and another does not. One dog hides when
little children come near while another allows children to
hang on him while they play. Our newest dog, Angel, likes to
tease the other dogs. Each has a different personality.

Spirit

The word *spirit* (*ruach* in Hebrew) means "wind, breath—
the living power of God's will at work." The spirit is the essence and will of God given to all humans and animals.

God put His spirit within all animals. Let's look at Ecclesiastes 3:18-21 TEV; Ecclesiastes 3:21 NAB; Wisdom 12:1
NJB; and Numbers 16:22 KJV).

> *I decided that God is testing us, to show us that we are no*
> *better than animals. After all, the same fate awaits man*
> *and animal alike. One dies just like the other. They are the*
> *same kind of creature. A human being is no better off than*
> *an animal, because life has no meaning for either. They are*

both going to the same place—the dust. They both came from it; they will both go back to it. How can anyone be sure that a man's spirit goes upward while an animal's spirit goes down into the ground? (Ecclesiastes 3:18-21 TEV).

Who knows if the life-breath of the children of men goes upward and the life-breath of beasts goes earthward? (Ecclesiastes 3:21 NAB).

For your imperishable spirit is in everything! (Wisdom 12:1 NJB).

And they fell upon their faces, and said, O God, the God of the spirits of all flesh, shall one man sin, and wilt thou be wroth with all the congregation? (Numbers 16:22 KJV).

The Scriptures say that man is born with a sinful nature (soul). Both the Old and New Testaments say that God put the knowledge of Himself within the heart (soul) of all mankind; thus, we have no excuse to reject Him or say we do not know who God is. (See Hebrews 10:15-16 KJV; Romans 1:18-23 KJV.) Remember, the animals also have a spirit from God, and because they are sinless, they have remained attached to God.

Although we can know the soul of man and animals, we cannot know the spirit of either. The spirits of animals and the elect angels have never been separated from God. As recorded in the Book of Numbers, animals can recognize spirit-beings and their spirits are tuned into the wisdom of God.

In the Book of Wisdom, one of the Apocrypha books that deals extensively with the reward of justice, God's mercy, and the folly of idolatry, we learn that God's eternal Spirit is in every living thing. It says: "For your imperishable spirit is in everything!" (Wisdom 12:1 NJB). Ecclesiastes 3:21 raises the question, "Where does the spirit of man and animals go?" We find the answer in Romans 8:21 of the King James Version of the Bible, when it states that the irrational creatures wait for the sons/children of God to have their bodies redeemed, to be freed from physical bondage.

The soul exists within a temporal plane, the world in which all creatures physically live. The soul is conscious of the passage of time and is aware of impending physical death. The spirit (which we sometimes describe as the wind or breath), on the other hand, is not temporal. The spirit can be above or below the temporal plane. Eternity is non-temporal, or timeless.

Because we can only relate well to the physical world in which we now live, we cannot easily understand timelessness. But to the spirit, time does not exist. Because of man's original sin, we cannot describe or understand the spirit, and because man has dominion over the animals, they must wait for our redemption in order to receive their liberty from this condemned world. (See Romans 8:21 KJV.) The Bible also says: "While we look not at the things which are seen, but at the things which are not seen: for the things which are seen *are* temporal; but the things which are not seen *are* eternal" (II Corinthians 4:18 KJV). The Holy Spirit links man back up with God and the rest of nature; with the animals that are at peace with the world; with living, dying, and eternity. The temporal plane, filled with guilt and fear, does not consume the lesser animals. They live predominantly on a non-temporal, or spiritual plane. Their innocent nature allows them to be free of guilt from the past and fear of the future; they have contentment. This does not mean that animals do not know fear and are not, at times, literally "scared stiff." It simply means they live in a state of forgiveness which allows them freedom from a constant fear of mortality. Nor does it mean that they do not feel guilt, for they do, but it does not appear to consume them.

The Books of Job and Sirach (both referred to as the Wisdom Books in the Catholic Bible) tell us that God holds the soul of every living thing in His hand. God has dominion over both His lesser creatures and man. All souls belong to Him and God can do with all His creatures whatever He chooses. The Book of Job says:

Who knoweth not in all these that the hand of the Lord hath wrought this? In whose hand is the soul of every living thing, and the breath of all mankind (Job 12:9-10 KJV).

The soul and spirit of the lesser creatures return to the face of God when the flesh returns to the earth as they await their new bodies along with God's children. The Book of Sirach says: "After this God looked upon the earth, and filled it with his goods. The soul of every living thing hath shown forth before the face thereof, and into it they return again" (Sirach 16:30-31 New Catholic Edition).

In *The Immortality of Animals*, Dr. E.D. Buckner quotes Reverend Dr. E.F. Bush:

"The phrase 'living soul' is repeatedly applied to the inferior order of animals. It would seem to mean the same when spoken of man that it does when spoken of beasts, viz, an animated being, a creature possessed of life and sensation, and capable of performing all the physical functions by which life is distinguished, and we find no terms in the Bible to distinguish the intellectual faculties of man from the brute creatures."[10]

Dr. Buckner, in his book *The Immortality of Animals* states:

"The Bible, without the shadow of a doubt, recognizes that animals have living souls the same as man. Most of the quotations given are represented as having been spoken by the Creator Himself, and He certainly knows whether or not He gave to man and the lower animals alike a living soul, which of course means an immortal soul...."[11]

The following story gives us a glimpse into the mind, wisdom, and spiritual understanding of the lesser creatures, and the pain they feel when they lose one of their own. It illustrates beautifully the spiritual and compassionate realm of the lesser animals.

Merrylegs Had a Foal

Merrylegs is a horse that belonged to a wonderful family, the Jensens, who live in St. Louis, Missouri. They have a large farm, about 50 miles south of St. Louis, where they keep cattle and some beautiful horses. Merrylegs was a Tennessee walking horse that was expecting her first foal. When the time came for her to deliver, Mr. and Mrs. Jensen went down to the farm to wait for the birth. Soon a beautiful little female foal was born. Everyone was very excited about the new foal, but their excitement turned into concern when they noticed that, despite its best efforts, the newborn couldn't nurse. Finally, Mrs. Jensen decided to put some of Merrylegs' milk into a bottle and feed the foal herself. But as hard as the foal tried, she could not drink the milk. Mr. Jensen called the veterinarian, who said that it sounded like "sleepy or dummy foal syndrome," a condition that occurs when a foal simply cannot take in anything but air. Foals with this condition are very healthy when they are inside the mother, but once they are born, they cannot take in food. Therefore, they soon die.

When Mr. Jensen returned after speaking with the veterinarian, he found his wife sitting on the floor of the barn with the little foal. She had placed hay all around to keep the newborn warm against the March cold. As Mrs. Jensen sat holding the little foal, Merrylegs came over to look at it again. Mrs. Jensen saw tears in the regal mare's eyes. Tearfully, Mrs. Jensen said, "I don't think your baby is going to live." Merrylegs looked on for a moment, then turned around and walked to the other side of the barn. She never again looked back at her foal.

Mrs. Jensen stayed with the mare and her foal all day long. That evening, the baby horse simply stopped breathing. At that instant, the Jensen's five other horses, which had over the past few hours gathered themselves as close to the barn as possible, reared up on their hind legs and gave several piercing screams. They could not have seen the foal because it was in the barn when it died—yet they knew. It was an experience Mrs. Jensen will never forget and, in this earthly life, she will never fully understand.

The experience Mrs. Jensen witnessed simply cannot be fully understood by the wisdom of natural man. However, it does testify to the reality of the soul and spirit God imparted to His lesser creatures.

Animals are in tune with nature; they can tell if a storm is coming even if they are inside the house. They have saved many people from disaster, made their way back home through unbelievable odds, sacrificed themselves to save their masters, and warned us of danger. Canines are used to help police locate drugs and track murderers. They also have become indispensable to the handicapped. In fact, dogs' senses are so keen that a bloodhound's testimony will actually hold up in a court of law.

Animals have spiritual knowledge and can communicate in ways man cannot comprehend. Through Scripture we know that God communicates with animals and in many cases uses them to communicate with us. We have heard many accounts of people who, having died and returned, saw Jesus. Many of them also saw animals and some, in fact, saw their own pets in Heaven. So animals can reason and recognize spirit entities. They experience fear and joy, and respond to the loss of people and other animals. Sometimes things occur in completely unexplained ways that man has been unable, through the natural world, to understand. My dog Duffy is a case in point.

Beagle to Beagle

Our pet beagle, Duffy, frequently visited our neighbors' beagle, Linus Jeziorski. Linus had an overbite, buggy eyes, and a bobbed tail. Because he stopped off almost every day to eat at four different neighbors' homes, he was, to say the least, a bit overweight. However, Linus did take time out from his rigorous eating routine to spend time with Duffy.

Duffy and Linus visited each other almost every day for more than 10 years. Duffy would drop over to the Jeziorski's house, push the screen door open, and simply walk in as though he owned the place. In fact, one morning after Mr. Jeziorski had taken his oldest son to school, he came back home to find Duffy in bed with his wife. Both were sound asleep. Mrs. "J," as my sons lovingly called her, had no idea that she was sleeping with a hound dog.

Duffy and Linus played together, ate together, and sometimes plotted together. Once they tried to evict an intruding Chinese pug that had come to town with his California masters for a short visit with the Jeziorskis. Four very amused adults observed the attack which took the dogs all day to plan. As usual, Duffy had arrived at 9:00 in the morning to visit Mr. and Mrs. J and Linus. When he arrived, he encountered the threatening canine intruder from California. Duffy and Linus went out under the tree in the backyard to "discuss" the matter. They looked at each other for awhile, then looked off into space for a period of time, then turned to look at each other again in order to contemplate their options.

Eventually, both dogs decided to reenter the house and put their plan into action. Linus was much too overweight to do any aggressive maneuvers, so he walked a short distance behind Duffy as they circled around the living room, through the dining room, past the bedrooms, and back through the living room, where this monstrous Chinese pug had perched himself on the divan between Mr. J and its owner. Duffy and Linus slowed down to stare at the pug, then walked slowly through the house before returning again to walk threateningly close to the divan.

This maneuver continued throughout the day, with short intermissions when Linus and Duffy would return to their post under the tree to further contemplate the situation. They knew this wrinkled invader had to go—the house certainly was not big enough for both Linus and the pug.

Once again, Linus and Duffy pushed the screen door open and began their walking vigil, waiting for just the right sign, just the right excuse to launch an all-out attack. Finally, at 6:00 in the evening, the perfect opportunity presented itself. As Duffy passed the divan on which the intruder had comfortably bedded himself in Mr. J's lap, he heard a growl from the pug. Claiming self-defense, Duffy lunged for him with all his might. He got a good hold and was quite proud of himself, but upon studying the victim, Duffy realized he had attached his mouth not to the pug's scruff, but to Mr. J's arm. The pug had scurried up to Mr. J's shoulder and was safely out of reach.

Needless to say, Duffy was brought back home and placed under yard arrest until the visitor returned to California. Mr. J was not hurt in the attack and the Jeziorskis were not upset with Duffy. They were, in fact, amazed and entertained at the planning and communication that took place between Linus and Duffy.

Duffy and Linus remained steadfast friends until Linus departed this world. When Linus died, Duffy never again went to visit the Jeziorski house. I have no idea how Duffy knew Linus was no longer there. He must have understood through the spiritual realm.

Scripture reveals that angels are independent thinkers, yet they live in obedience to God. So why should it surprise us that animals live in obedience to God's will, and possibly understand things that we, the spiritually blinded, cannot see?

There are many, many accounts of animals that have demonstrated spiritual knowledge and understanding beyond what the natural man can comprehend. It is truly awe-inspiring to see a glimpse of God's wisdom and the magnificence in which He created all His creatures. Having had Duffy as a wonderful friend for more than 17 years, I have recognized many times in which he had seen beyond my human understanding. It seems selfish that we of the human race feel that of all creation, we should be the only creatures of any eternal importance.

All Return to Dust

In the Book of Revelation, which speaks of a time yet to come when God will remove all sin from the world, one of God's angels will physically destroy every living creature in the sea. It says: "And the second angel poured out his vial upon the sea; and it became as the blood of a dead *man*: and every living soul died in the sea" (Revelation 16:3 KJV).

As we read Ecclesiastes 3:18-21 in The Living Bible, we find that although God will judge the good and evil things man does, like the animals, man will return to dust. The Bible says:

And then I realized that God is letting the world go on its sinful way so that he can test mankind, and so that men themselves will see that they are no better than beasts. For men and animals both breathe the same air, and both die. So mankind has no real advantage over the beasts; what an absurdity! All go to one place—the dust from which they came and to which they must return. For who can prove that the spirit of man goes upward and the spirit of animals goes downward into dust? (Ecclesiastes 3:18-21 TLB).

Some say that the spirit of man goes upward and the spirit of animals goes downward upon physical death. The Bible, however, does not support that theory. In Ecclesiastes of The Living Bible 3:11-21, Solomon raised this question to stimulate thinking as he searched for God's wisdom. "Everything is appropriate in its own time. But though God has planted eternity in the hearts of men, even so, man cannot see the whole scope of God's work from beginning to end" (Ecclesiastes 3:11 TLB). From dust all life comes and to dust all life returns. As for the spirit of man and of animal, where does it go? The Scriptures are not saying that the spirit of man goes upward. God's Word does not say that all human spirits go upward to Heaven; nor does it say that animals' spirits go downward. The real issue is the value of existence on earth and its worthlessness without God. All is not fair and just in this life. The real purpose of life is to show trust and faith in our Creator and give obedience to Him as we plan for the perfection of the next world. The Book of Job says:

Who doesn't know that the Lord does things like that? Ask the dumbest beast—he knows that it is so; ask the birds—they will tell you; or let the earth teach you, or the fish of the sea. For the soul of every living thing is in the hand of God, and the breath of all mankind (Job 12:7-10 TLB).

The Bible also says:

There before me lies the mighty ocean, teeming with life of every kind, both great and small. And look! See the ships! And over there, the whale you made to play in the sea. Every one of these depends on you to give them daily food. You supply it, and they gather it. You open wide your hand to feed them and they are satisfied with all your bountiful provision. But if you turn away from them, then all is lost. And when you gather up their breath, they die and turn again to dust. Then you send your Spirit, and new life is born to replenish all the living of the earth. Praise God forever! How he must rejoice in all his work! The earth trembles at his glance; the mountains burst into flame at his touch" (Psalm 104:25-32 TLB).

Bishop Joseph Butler (1692-1752) noted: "We cannot argue from the reason of the thing that death is the destruction of living agents. Nor can we find anything throughout the whole analogy of nature to afford us even the slightest presumption that animals ever lose their living powers, much less, if it were possible, that they lose them by death."[12]

Raised Presbyterian, Bishop Butler joined the Church of England, became rector, bishop, then dean of St. Paul's. In

The Analogy of Religion, Bishop Butler became one of the first clergymen to teach the immortality of animal souls.

Dr. Buckner says, "If by the original sin of man all animals were affected in the fall, and if by the atonement of Christ man is affected in the restoration, certainly lower animals are likewise affected. Now, under the first Adam, lower animals were created without death or sin, but fell with man; so in the final destiny they will be restored with man under the second Adam, for 'as in Adam all die, so in Christ shall all be made alive.' "[13]

He also spoke concerning the spirit: "When a man communicates his ideas it must be through a spiritual mode, for matter or material substance cannot communicate with the soul or immaterial essence; consequently animals must have an immaterial nature or soul the same as man."

Animals as Symbols

In the Bible, God sometimes used animals to describe to man the consequences of sin. Since we did not see animals in their original state (before man sinned), we do not understand why God made each animal the way He did.

Consider the poisonous snake. We are terrified of it because its bite can kill us. Of all the animals in the animal kingdom, snakes are looked upon as demons. God put that curse on them. (We'll discuss this in greater depth in Chapter VI.) But let's look at the value they might have had before sin entered the world. According to Dr. Baugh of the Creation Evidences Museum in Texas, snake venom is almost pure protein. Today we get most of our protein from eating meat. Before man sinned, no animal died; therefore, there was no meat. All creatures ate seeds and grain before the fall of man. Perhaps the snake supplied us with the protein we needed.

After man sinned, all of nature took on a new disposition. Animals had to fear man—the trust between man and animals was broken.

And God blessed Noah and his sons, and said unto them, Be fruitful, and multiply, and replenish the earth. And the fear of you and the dread of you shall be upon every beast of the earth, and upon every fowl of the air, upon all that moveth upon *the earth, and upon all the fishes of the sea; into your hand are they delivered. Every moving thing that liveth shall be meat for you; even as the green herb have I given you all things* (Genesis 9:1-3 KJV).

Using such techniques as symbolism, parables, imagery, and word pictures to describe bad people, good people, cultures, countries, etc., is one of the easiest ways to get a point across. It is also a way of breaking the language barrier. Without God's unique use of animals and their various dispositions and habits, there might not have been a way for the Bible and all the messages included in it to be transposed and understood. Without symbolism, the Bible might not have retained its meaning throughout centuries.

We can recognize the style in which the writers used various animals in the Scriptures. For instance, some writers, when referring to an animal, literally meant that animal. In the Books of Daniel and Revelation, however, most of the references to any form of animals are symbolic. Isaiah, too, contains a great deal of symbolism. The symbolism used by these writers is very different, however. These differences are quite fascinating. When reading the Old Testament, we must realize that wild animals harmed many people and ungodly men did likewise. This is why the Scriptures are always comparing wild animals to evil men. God gave His people permission to kill both. In fact, at times God commanded man to kill tribes of people with their children, animals, and all living beings under their domain. In the Book of Isaiah, jackals and owls were used to represent non-Jewish people.

During the time the Old Testament was written, dogs were regarded by Jews as dirty, unclean, predatory scavengers. They became a symbol of worthlessness and uncleanness. Also during that time, the Gentiles were regarded by

Jews as not being worthy of human status. They were considered unclean, uncircumcised wild beasts—dogs. They were not God's chosen people; thus, they were thought to be of little value. In one encounter, Jesus indicates how the Gentiles were thought of during the Old Testament times. In Mark 7:24-30 (KJV), a Gentile woman is compared to a dog. Although the Jews were the chosen people, because of her humility, faith and hope, Jesus drove out the demon from her child.

Gentiles today are viewed much differently. Some Gentiles have been adopted into God's Kingdom through Jesus Christ. We are God's adopted children. Because of Jesus Christ, we can become God's chosen people. However, there are still Gentiles who hate others, who follow Satan, who are murderers, idolaters, and whoremongers, etc. The Book of Revelation refers to these evil people as dogs. It says: "For without *are* dogs, and sorcerers, and whoremongers, and murderers, and idolaters, and whosoever loveth and maketh a lie" (Revelation 22:15 KJV).

The Scriptures say that man can tame the beasts, or lower creatures, of the earth but man cannot be tamed because of his tongue. The Book of James says: "For every kind of beasts, and of birds, and of serpents, and of things in the sea, is tamed, and hath been tamed of mankind: But the tongue can no man tame; *it is* an unruly evil, full of deadly poison" (James 3:7-8 KJV). The writers of Scripture, over and over, came to use the word *beast* to refer to man. "Beast" may be referring to barbaric man, Gentiles, Satan, and at times, real animals.

In First Corinthians 15:32 (TLB), the wild beasts symbolically mean men. It says:

And what value was there in fighting wild beasts—those men of Ephesus—if it was only for what I gain in this life down here? If we will never live again after we die, then we might as well go and have ourselves a good time: let us eat, drink,

*and be merry. What's the difference? For tomorrow we die,
and that ends everything!* (1 Corinthians 15:32 TLB).

Probably the most misunderstood word in the Bible referring to animals other than the word *soul* is the word *perish*. In reading Dr. Buckner's book, I found a most interesting truth. The word has long been questioned concerning Second Peter 2:12 when it speaks of natural brute beasts that perish.

In Dr. Buckner's research on the word *perish*, he discovered the word could not be found in the original Hebrew and so should not be added. The Jewish Bible, when referring to brute beasts, says: "like the beasts that are irrational." It does not mean the annihilation of lower animals or man. The meaning intended is that they will be forgotten. In other words, the rich and wicked man may perish or die and his name be forgotten like a beast that dies and is forgotten. An example of the word *perish* would be when His disciples spoke to Jesus in the storm, saying, "Lord, save us: we perish" (Matthew 8:25 KJV).

The Book of Daniel is rich in symbolism. Four beasts coming out of the sea represent four kingdoms, as Daniel saw them in a dream. One kingdom visually appeared as a lion with the wings of an eagle; the second beast looked like a bear; the third beast looked like a leopard with four wings like a bird, and had four heads; while the fourth beast was the most terrifying of all, as it had 10 horns and one horn with the eyes of men and a mouth that spoke boastfully. In his dream, God, who was known as "the Ancient of days," came and sat down in His seat. Then came Jesus—the Son of man out of Heaven—and God gave Him the power to rule all creation forever. (See Daniel 7:2-9,11,17-18 KJV). Another vision Daniel had, one about the ram and the goat, occurred during the third year of King Belshazzar's reign. The Book of Daniel says: "I saw the ram pushing westward, and northward, and southward; so that no beasts might stand before

him, neither *was there any* that could deliver out of his hand;
but he did according to his will, and became great" (Daniel
8:4 KJV). The two-horned ram represents the kings of Media
and Persia. The shaggy goat is the king of Greece. "And as I
was considering, behold, an he goat came from the west on
the face of the whole earth, and touched not the ground:
and the goat *had* a notable horn between his eyes" (Daniel
8:5 KJV).

The Bible is full of symbolism. God uses animals to communicate His message to people in an ageless manner. The
following stories, as told by a friend Lou, a wonderful Christian, allow us to get a glimpse of what so many have, until
now, only hoped for concerning the eternal destination of
their beloved pets.

Butchie

*Butchie was a small terrier-mix. He was a snow-white
puppy when we picked him up at the pound. He was "full of the
old nick" from the day he came home with us, and I loved him
very much.*

*He loved to run, chase squirrels and birds, dig up moles (or
at least try to), eat, and sleep with me. Every night, when he
would see me heading for bed, he would run down the hall and
jump onto the bed. After I would get into bed, he would grunt
and squirm around on the bed until he got as close to me as he
could. He was a wonderful little bed partner and helped keep
me warm on cold winter nights.*

*When he was about 12, I began noticing that something was
wrong with him. I wasn't sure if he was having seizures or a
stroke. But he would lose his balance, sway back and forth, and
sometimes fall. It was heartbreaking, as I knew that sooner or
later, he was going to leave me. After about six months or so, I
knew that the time had come to put him to sleep.*

*I couldn't bear to take him to the vet myself, so I called a
very good friend and asked him to do it for me. I didn't even
want to be there when my friend picked Butchie up to take him.*

I told him that I wouldn't be home around 11:00 a.m. and could he please come and get him at that time. Butchie and I snuggled together on the couch that morning and I said my last good-byes to him. It was very, very sad and difficult. I left the house in tears, knowing that when I returned, Butchie wouldn't be there.

I didn't really know when my friend was coming to get him, but about 12:30 p.m. or so, I was still away from home. All of a sudden, out of nowhere, I had this vision—a mental picture.

My mom had passed away about a year earlier; she was a Christian, and I knew she was in Heaven. In my vision, I saw Butchie fly through the air into the arms of my mom who had a very surprised look on her face. It was almost as if she was saying, "What are you doing here, Butch?" Nonetheless, she caught him. Butchie had crossed over from this life into the next, right into the arms of my mom.

Later that afternoon, I asked my friend what time he took Butchie to the veterinarian, and he said about 12:00. The time of my vision, 12:30, was just about the time when Butchie had been put to sleep. I can't wait to see my mom and Butchie in Heaven!

Tribute to Theresa and Cotton

I inherited my love for animals from my mom. Even though we lived in suburban areas, we always had a lot of animals— dogs, cats, and occasionally ducks, chickens, and parakeets. Even though mom loved all animals, she was especially fond of dogs. Though she loved every one of her dogs, her favorite was Cotton.

Cotton was a mixed breed from one of the animal shelters in our town. He was predominantly golden Lab, and he had a wonderful temperament. Because he had cancer, Cotton had to be put to sleep when he was about 10 years old. That was very, very difficult for my mother, and it hurt her deeply to put him to sleep.

I had a dream one night that I'll never forget. My mom had passed away from emphysema about nine months earlier. I was still very much in grief, even though my grief was lessened by the fact that I know I will see my mom again in Heaven because my mom had a personal relationship with Jesus Christ, as I do.

Because I love animals I, too, loved Cotton very much. I certainly hadn't thought about him for over a year, though. He had been put to sleep at least 10 years before mom passed away.

In my dream, I was in a room filled with people and it seemed like a party. Then, all of a sudden, my mom appeared in the room. In the dream I knew that mom had passed away and had just come back for a visit. Her appearance didn't scare me at all, as I was overjoyed to see her. She looked wonderful. I said something like, "Mom, it's so good to see you!" At first my eyes were only on mom. But all of a sudden, I looked down to mom's left, and there was her precious Cotton. He also looked great!

My interpretation of the dream was this: Mom and Cotton were together in Heaven and had come back just for a visit—to say "hi." How good it was to see them! What a treat in the midst of my grief!

"The Holy Scriptures," The Jewish Publication Society of America, 1917 says: and to every beast of the earth, and to every fowl of the air, and to every thing that creepeth upon the earth, wherein there is a living soul, I have given every green herb for food.' And it was so. (Genesis 1:30)

And they went in unto Noah into the ark. two and two of all flesh wherein is the breath of life. (Genesis 7:15)

And all flesh perished that moved upon the earth, both fowl, and cattle, and beast and every swarming thing that swarmeth upon the earth, and every man; 22 all in whose nostrils was the breath of the spirit of life, what-soever was in the dry land, died.

(Genesis 7:21-22)

Chapter III

Obedience and Wisdom

Who endowed the ibis with wisdom and gave the cock his intelligence? (Job 38:36 NJB).

Happy is *the man* that *findeth wisdom, and the man* that *getteth understanding* (Proverbs 3:13 KJV).

Spiritual Wisdom

Animals obey God and are full of His wisdom. God demands obedience from all His Kingdom, including the animals. Wisdom is the highest form of knowledge. It comes from the Spirit and, according to the Scriptures, God gives wisdom to all His creatures. When I use the word *wisdom*, I am not referring to human intellect or feelings. Although we often refer to human wisdom in our everyday language, it is clearly different from the spiritual wisdom, or insight, that God gives to the lesser animals and His elect angels, and offered to humans through the Holy Spirit and the Scriptures. It is important to learn that humans can obtain spiritual wisdom, or "wisdom of the soul," but unlike animals, are not born with it. The Bible says: "Yea, the stork in the heaven knoweth her appointed times; and the turtle and the crane and the swallow observe the time of their coming; but my people know not the judgment of the Lord" (Jeremiah 8:7 KJV). This chapter explains both animals' obedience to God and the wisdom they have through their spiritual connection with God, using both the Scriptures and stories.

Obedience

In the story of Balaam, his donkey talked. Not many animals talk in ways that we can understand (except for some birds that learn to mimic man), so animals are referred to in the Bible as being "dumb." (See Second Peter 2:16 KJV.) In the New International Version of the Bible, the word *mute* (voiceless by nature or choice) is used instead of dumb. (See Isaiah 56:10 NIV.)

In the story of Balaam, Balaam's donkey obeyed the angel of God. When the Israelites were entering the land of Canaan, Balak, the Moabite king, feared the Israelites and called for the soothsayer Balaam to put a curse on them. God told Balaam not to curse the Israelites but Balak made Balaam an offer he couldn't refuse. Balaam was determined to disobey God, so God let him disobey, to teach him a lesson. Only the obedience of Balaam's donkey and God's mercy saved Balaam from being killed.

Following is the story according to the Scriptures:

And God came unto Balaam at night, and said unto him, If the men come to call thee, rise up, and go with them, but yet the word which I shall say unto thee, that shalt thou do. And Balaam rose up in the morning, and saddled his ass, and went with the princes of Moab. And God's anger was kindled because he went: and the angel of the Lord stood in the way for an adversary against him. Now he was riding upon his ass, and his two servants were with him. And the ass saw the angel of the Lord standing in his way, and his sword drawn in his hand: and the ass turned aside out of the way, and went into the field: and Balaam smote the ass, to turn her into the way. But the angel of the Lord stood in a path of the vineyards, a wall being on this side, and a wall on that side. And when the ass saw the angel of the Lord, she thrust herself unto the wall, and crushed Balaam's foot against the wall: and he smote her again.

And the angel of the Lord went further, and stood in a narrow place, where was no way to turn either to the right hand or to the left. And when the ass saw the angel of the Lord, she fell down under Balaam: and Balaam's anger was kindled, and he smote the ass with a staff. And the Lord opened the mouth of the ass, and she said unto Balaam, What have I done unto thee, that thou hast smitten me these three times? And Balaam said unto the ass, Because thou hast mocked me: I would there were a sword in mine hand, for now would I kill thee. And the ass said unto Balaam, Am not I thine ass, upon which thou hast ridden ever since I was thine unto this day? was I ever wont to do so unto thee? And he said, Nay. Then the Lord opened the eyes of Balaam, and he saw the angel of the Lord standing in the way, and his sword drawn in his hand: and he bowed down his head, and fell flat on his face. And the angel of the Lord said unto him, Wherefore hast thou smitten thine ass these three times? behold, I went out to withstand thee, because thy *way is perverse before me: And the ass saw me, and turned from me these three times: unless she had turned from me, surely now also I had slain thee, and saved her alive* (Numbers 22:20-33 KJV).

In the story of Jonah, we see Jonah simply refusing to do what God told him to do. So God called upon one of His creatures to get Jonah's attention. Jonah was a prophet who forecast the growth of Israel under the reign of Jeroboam II. God chose Jonah to warn the Assyrians (the Ninevites) of a planned invasion from a hostile neighbor. Jonah, however, *wanted* the Assyrians to be attacked, so he did not want to obey God's command. When Jonah decided to flee by boat from God, God caused Jonah to be thrown out of the boat and swallowed by a great fish to teach him a lesson. Later, Jonah disobeyed God again. (He wasn't the most cooperative of prophets.)

To understand Jonah's plight in running from God and the consequences of his disobedience, read the Book of Jonah. The following are key verses from it: "Now the Lord had prepared a great fish to swallow up Jonah. And Jonah was in the belly of the fish three days and three nights" (Jonah 1:17 KJV). Jonah found himself in the belly of the whale as a punishment from God. I am not sure the whale was at all happy about the situation, but at least it was obeying God. The story of Jonah goes on:

> *Then Jonah prayed unto the Lord his God out of the fish's belly, And said, I cried by reason of mine affliction unto the Lord, and he heard me; out of the belly of hell cried I, and thou heardest my voice. ... And the Lord spake unto the fish, and it vomited out Jonah upon the dry land* (Jonah 2:1-2,10 KJV).

In Jonah 3:1-10, both the people and the animals are fasting and wearing sackcloth to keep God's wrath from coming. These sinful people are repenting, and even the animals have to dress up and fast to help get out of another one of man's messes. The Book of Jonah says:

> *And Jonah began to enter into the city a day's journey, and he cried, and said, Yet forty days, and Nineveh shall be overthrown. So the people of Nineveh believed God, and proclaimed a fast, and put on sackcloth, from the greatest of them even to the least of them. For word came unto the king of Nineveh, and he arose from his throne, and he laid his robe from him, and covered him with sackcloth, and sat in ashes. And he caused it to be proclaimed and published through Nineveh by the decree of the king and his nobles, saying, Let neither man nor beast, herd nor flock, taste any thing, let them not feed, nor drink water: But let man and beast be covered with sackcloth, and cry mightily unto God: yea, let them turn every one from his evil way, and from the violence that is in their hands* (Jonah 3:4-8 KJV).

God, it seems, requires obedience from the highest members of the household (man), to the lowest members (the animal kingdom).

God gave Moses the Ten Commandments on Mount Sinai. Through them, God laid out the laws man was to obey. Moses, believed to be the writer of Exodus and Deuteronomy, mentioned in both books a day of rest for both man and the animals. The fourth commandment tells man, as well as the animals that work for him, to rest on the seventh day. God created the world in six days and rested on the seventh. The seventh day is for rest and praise to God, the Creator. The physical body needs to rest one out of every seven days in order to be refreshed.

The Book of Exodus says:

Remember the Sabbath day and keep it holy. For six days you shall labour and do all your work, but the seventh day is a Sabbath for Yahweh your God. You shall do no work that day, neither you nor your son nor your daughter nor your servants, men or women, nor your animals nor the alien living with you (Exodus 20:8-11 NJB).

Deuteronomy says:

Keep the sabbath day to sanctify it, as the Lord thy God hath commanded thee. Six days thou shalt labour, and do all thy work: But the seventh day is *the sabbath of the Lord thy God:* in it *thou shalt not do any work, thou, nor thy son, nor thy daughter, nor thy manservant, nor thy maidservant, nor thine ox, nor thine ass, nor any of thy cattle, nor thy stranger that* is *within thy gates; that thy manservant and thy maidservant may rest as well as thou* (Deuteronomy 5:12-14 KJV).

Wisdom

God told Job about the wisdom and dispositions of His lesser creatures. The Book of Job (chapters 38 through 41), and Psalms (Psalms 145 and 148), contain fascinating revelations of the knowledge and uniqueness God put into each of His lesser creatures. God made all creation good; Satan, through man, corrupted God's creation for a time. But all creatures will live and remain forever.

Godly wisdom is given by God and it imparts knowledge into the soul. In man, it is characterized by humility, hard work, uprightness, and concern for others. Some animals possess these types of characteristics. Proverbs 6:6-8 gives evidence of the practical knowledge of the ant: "Go to the ant, you sluggard; consider its ways and be wise! It has no commander, no overseer or ruler, yet it stores its provisions in summer and gathers its food at harvest" (Proverbs 6:6-8 NIV).

The Scriptures say that man and animals are to look to God. They are to fear Him. (To God, "fear" means honor and reverence.) The following Scriptures explain that God poured wisdom out upon all His works (creation). God has given a unique understanding and intelligence to all His creatures. We will not fully understand God's complete wisdom concerning His creation until we get to Heaven. The Book of Sirach says:

> *All wisdom is from the Lord God, and hath been always with him, and is before all time. Who hath searched out the wisdom of God that goeth before all things? Wisdom hath been created before all things, and the understanding of prudence from everlasting. There is one most high Creator Almighty, and a powerful king, and greatly to be feared, who sitteth upon his throne, and is the God of dominion. He created her in the Holy Ghost, and saw her, and numbered her, and measured her. And he poured her out upon all his works, and upon all flesh according to his gift, and hath given her to them that love him* (Sirach 1:1,3-4,8-10 New Catholic Edition).

Following is an example of the wisdom of some of God's little creatures. The conies mentioned in Proverbs 30:26 are rabbit-sized animals that resemble guinea pigs. They live in Africa and southwestern Asia, and are related to the hoofed animals. Conies live in rocky hills or in trees; their cry sounds like an agonized screech. The Book of Proverbs says:

> *There be four* things which are *little upon the earth, but they* are *exceeding wise: The ants* are *a people not strong, yet they prepare their meat in the summer; The conies* are but *a feeble folk, yet make they their houses in the rocks; The locusts have no king, yet go they forth all of them by bands; The spider taketh hold with her hands, and is in king's palaces* (Proverbs 30:24-28 KJV).

The ibis is a wading bird. White ibis birds are found in southern United States. The sacred ibis birds of Egypt are black and white. The beautiful cock of the rock is a South American bird. This bird lives in rocky ravines near mountain streams in the Andes from Colombia to Bolivia. Some are found in the mountains of the Guianas and northern Brazil. During mating season the male birds gather together in a cleared spot in the forest and dance around to attract the females. They make their nests of plant fibers, which they glue together with resin and stick to crevices of the rocks.

> *Who endowed the ibis with wisdom and gave the cock his intelligence?* (Job 38:36 NJB).

Though God has made each kind of bird unique, I have found the common crow to be truly fascinating. My brother, Mac Allen, brought a crow he named Jim into my world when I was about seven years old. Jim was one of the most interesting creatures I have ever known. Through our pet crow, God allowed our family to see true wisdom and reasoning. We also learned the unique humor God puts into some of His creatures and, unfortunately, how trust in humans can sometimes bring them harm.

Life with Jim

Mac was a teenager when he found a nest of crows on our
family farm. Since he had always heard that crows make wonderful pets and were quite intelligent, he waited for the eggs to
hatch and went in search of a baby crow. He found one and
named it Jim (we never knew for sure if Jim was really a Jim or
a Jenny, but we thought of him as Jim). Mac fed Jim bread and
milk and cut very small bits of meat from time to time to feed
the little bird.

Jim grew to be a very healthy and proud crow. He followed
us around the farm, either walking with us or flying above us.
He lived outside in a fir tree near the back door. Our dogs and
cats also loved the old fir tree and often slept underneath it.
When the dogs and cats were asleep, Jim would fly down, grab
a tail, pull on it, and then fly back up in the tree cawing victo-
riously, happy he'd made one of them angry. He loved every
minute of his troublemaking and would always wait until they
settled back down to sleep before starting the whole routine over
again.

Jim also loved hiding buttons and marbles. He spent a great
deal of time taking them from us and hiding them under leaves.
He would hide them, go off to play, or sit on our shoulder for
awhile, then frantically fly back to where he had buried them,
only to retrieve them and hide them somewhere else.

Jim's most humorous episodes occurred in the barn lot. He
liked to sit on a fence post and watch us milk the cows. Because
our cows were very gentle and would stand still for milking, my
dad was able to put them into the barn lot instead of the barn
stalls. Well, Jim discovered he could cause quite a ruckus and
have some fun harassing the cows in the barn lot while they
were being milked. He would wait until a cow had her back to
him and then would fly down from his attack position on the
fence post, grab the old cow's tail, brace his feet on the ground,
pull back on the tail, and hang on for dear life. Naturally, the
startled cow would take off running. Both the bucket of milk
and me, the milker, would go toppling backward while Jim flew

along for a bit. Then he would let go and sail up to the fence post, cawing for all he was worth. The cow and I would com- pose ourselves, only to have the same thing happen again as soon as Jim got the opportunity.

Crows can reason, as we found out one day when Mac brought Jim into the house. Jim flew around hiding bright but- tons, marbles, and anything else shiny he could get his beak on. In particular, he wanted to hide one shiny button under the edge of a throw rug. He set the button down near the rug and picked up the rug's corner with his beak to put the button under it. That was a great idea, but of course the rug flopped back over in place when he let go of it, before he could get the button underneath. Jim tried this procedure two times. The third time, Jim put the button down very close to the rug, picked up the rug's corner with his beak, put his foot on the rug to hold it in place, reached over and picked up the button with his beak, and laid it down where the corner of the rug would go. He then took his foot off of the rug. It flopped back over and covered the but- ton just as he planned. Jim went off to find another bright object to hide somewhere else.

Ironically, Jim's trust in us was his only real fault. Because of our friendship with him, he lost his sense of fear. One Sunday morning, we returned home from church and Jim wasn't in his tree. We knew that something was wrong. We called and called but Jim never returned. A few days later, we learned that he had been run over while sitting in the road. Jim was so much fun and he trusted us so much, it was very sad to be without him in our lives.

There is no doubt that Jim could think and solve prob- lems. He was just a wild crow, but like many of God's crea- tures, he had wisdom and a sense of humor. Sometimes we don't stop to realize just how intelligent all the birds we watch every day really are. God has given understanding to all His creatures.

The Bible is a vital source of spiritual wisdom. In conduct- ing the research for this book, however, I began to wonder how many times we may be reading the Bible for such selfish reasons, as: What Scriptures can I stand on to be financially blessed? to find favor with others? to prove to others I am right? and many other self-serving reasons—thereby missing its true power, insight, and wisdom. How many of us read the Bible to understand God's love for all His creation, for everything and everyone He has created? If we omit *self* from our thoughts as we read the Scriptures, we will have a closer walk with God. In humility, we will appreciate all of God's creation. We will treat His lesser creatures in humane ways without abuse or neglect, or unnecessary confinement of wild animals that were born to be free. We would stop the needless breeding of pets for profit when we already have many pets that cannot live out their earthly lives because of overpopulation in a world where they are unwanted. The use of animals for gaming (betting) and unnecessary experimentation demonstrates the condition of man's soul and the value he places on God's creation.

Consider this for a moment: A dog has somewhat the same mental and emotional capabilities of a three-year-old child. But, unlike a child, a dog cannot talk in ways we can understand, and it has no hands to do the things a child can do. Yet even with these limitations, a seeing-eye dog has the wisdom to learn to open doors, pick up items, make life-saving decisions, and be the eyes of its master.

The dog is able to do many things without hands that humans need their hands to do. A minister once told a true story about the importance of hands. He told of a fairly large animal in Africa that ate fruit from trees. It tried and tried to put more than one of the fruit in its mouth to take it back to its home, but each time one fruit would pop out of its mouth. Finally, it put one fruit in its mouth and kicked the other one with its hoof back to its home. Animals are very innovative indeed.

Animals also save other animals. I recently heard the story of a dog that saved another dog from drowning, and it was reported and printed in *Suburban Journal Newspapers*.[14]

Puppy Love

It was a clear-cut case of canine courage. Fritzle, a one-year-old schnauzer, might have drowned last Tuesday if it hadn't been for the dogged determination of his constant companion, Tonka, a beagle-mix that lives next door.

It was just past 8:00 a.m. when Carol McCoy heard her neighbor's dog at her back door. She figured Tonka, that routinely "knocks" at the back door, was in search of his playmate. "I heard him knocking and scratching at my back door and told him Fritzle was already outside," McCoy says. "But he just kept it up, so I even shut the door and told him to go home."

Undaunted, two-year-old Tonka, the family pet of Bill and Lynne Seebold, persisted in scratching and wheezing outside the McCoy's door. The dog's continued pestering worked. McCoy stuck her head outside and heard an unusual whining sound. "At first I thought it was some kind of bird, but then I realized it was Fritzle," McCoy says. "I couldn't find him, though, so I started calling his name. I thought maybe he had been bitten by a snake in the woods and was hurt."

McCoy soon realized the whining was coming from the swimming pool in her backyard. "We had a solar cover on the pool to keep the leaves out," she says. "When I pulled it back, I found Fritzle standing in the shallow end on his tiptoes, with just his nose sticking out of the water."

McCoy is convinced that Fritzle's canine companion saved his life. "If it hadn't been for Tonka pestering me, something might have happened to Fritzle. I don't know how long he could have stood on his hind legs like that."

The two neighbors admit that the story smacks of a Rin Tin Tin episode, but both are quick to point out that their pets are smarter than the average dog. "We call them 'the boys' because they're always hanging around together," McCoy says. "They're just like kids—always in trouble together."

The first one out in the morning races to the other dog's house and the two pets spend their dog days playing together in the Sunset Hills neighborhood, Lynne Seebold says. Grudgingly, McCoy admits that Tonka may have taken the lead in the intelligence category—at least, temporarily. "We have this running rivalry about who's the smartest dog in the neighborhood," McCoy says. "I think Tonka wins this week."

As Tonka and Fritzle illustrate, the feeling animals have for each other is very apparent. A friend of mine lost her cat because it grieved itself to death by not eating when she went away to college. This was a common occurrence during war time when men went away to war; their dogs would simply not eat and starved to death grieving for their masters.

The story, "Heidi," as told by Dr. Lana Richard, is one we are most familiar with. Animals, especially dogs, have an unexplained but spiritual wisdom to recognize when humans are in trouble. Dr. Richard tells her story:

Heidi

At the age of 37, I was diagnosed with diabetes. The doctors thought at first that oral medication, along with a healthy diet and exercise, would be enough to control the disease; however, this was not the case. After about six months, I was put on three injections a day. Having your body get used to the sudden "kick-in" of the insulin takes some time and adjustment. So with self-determination and the support of my husband, Bob, I began trying to deal with my newly-acquired health problem in addition to getting on with my life.

We were remodeling our kitchen and had several relatives and friends over to help us. Our German shepherd-mix dog, Heidi, loved all the attention she was getting as folks stopped every now and then to talk to her and laugh at her cute ways and tricks. I was in the midst of packing and storing when I realized I was having a low blood-sugar attack. I checked it on my monitor and, sure enough, it was at a reading of 75. I needed to stop and take a few minutes to eat something. I was just about to do that when I became distracted by another project that was going on and I completely forgot about my vulnerable condition. I don't know how long it was, somewhere between 20 minutes and an hour, when I realized I was really sick. "I've got to lie down right now," I said to myself.

I made it into the bedroom, unknown to anyone else, and laid on our bed. Although I could feel myself slipping into unconsciousness, I could hear everything that was going on: the men hammering in the kitchen, the phone ringing, people in the basement. I knew I was in trouble but I was just too weak to call out Bob's name, while sweating profusely. Then, my sweet little 45-pound dog—the one that had shown up at our doorstep about four years ago in the middle of an ice storm—jumped on the bed and began whining and licking my face. I was even too weak to push her off. She jumped down and I could hear her little feet on the kitchen floor where Bob and some of the men were working. She whined and then ran back into our bedroom and jumped on the bed and tried to lick me back into this world. After about five or six more licks, she jumped back down and ran into the kitchen where she stood and looked at Bob, whined, and then returned back to me. She repeated this behavior over and over. I finally heard Bob say, "Stop it, Heidi. Go find Lana and leave us alone." Then he paused and said, "By the way, where is Lana?" When she heard Bob say my name, Heidi ran into the hallway, stopped, and looked back at Bob. As he started toward our bedroom, she jumped on the bed and began whining and licking my face. Bob came over and realized what was wrong and said to Heidi, "It's okay, Heidi. I'll take care of her now." Heidi laid down right beside me and looked up at Bob with trusting eyes.

After working with me and giving me some of my glucose tablets that I carry with me in case of such an emergency, I came to and felt much better. I learned a huge lesson from the experience: whenever I feel a low blood-sugar attack coming on,

I need to take care of it as soon as possible. Now, whenever I lie down for a nap or get up in the middle of the night to lie on the couch, Heidi will come over and rouse me just to make certain I'm okay. I often laugh and tell people that Heidi is my "she can stay one night" dog. There was a time when I never would have let an animal in the house to live with us. To me, people who did that were just not clean. Well, now she sleeps at the foot of our bed, has the run of the house, and is part of our family.

"Rawhide Saves a Friend" is a true story of a horse communicating with a man to save one of his friends. It demonstrates the wisdom and communication skills of animals.

Rawhide Saves a Friend

The Jensens told me of the following remarkable experience, which happened to Jay Jensen as he was going out to the farm to check on the three horses they kept with their herd of cattle. Every evening when Jay checked on the horses, they always came when they heard him call. However, one particular evening none of the horses came. Finally, his son's little quarter horse, Rawhide, came part of the way to meet him, but turned around and ran back into the pasture where the brush was very thick. When Jay called a second and third time, Rawhide came part way again, then circled around and ran back into the pasture. Jay decided to follow Rawhide.

Rawhide ran ahead, turning around often to see if Jay was following. When the horse neared the large wooded area, he went behind a tree and started back into the brush. He hadn't gotten very far when Jay spotted an older horse caught in a barbed wire fence. She was caught in the corner of a fence row where a wire was sticking out and she was bleeding profusely from the hind quarters, which were tangled in the fence. She looked as though she had been there for at least a day. Jay was able to unroll the wire to free her.

The most remarkable part of the entire experience was the reaction of Rawhide. As Jay was freeing the injured horse, Rawhide put his head on the back of the trapped mare and

continued to make low moaning sounds as he watched Jay work
to free her. As soon as the older mare was free, both of the horses
took off through the brush and ran out into the open pasture like
two little children, while Jay phoned for medical assistance.

God's divine love made communication possible in the
form of sign, or body language. This is the language through
which many animals understand humans, but through which
few humans understand animals. The story demonstrates
God's loving grace even among His lower creatures. The
Psalms say:

Yahweh, your faithful love is in the heavens, your constancy
reaches to the clouds, your saving justice is like towering
mountains, your judgements like the mighty deep. Yahweh,
you support both man and beast (Psalm 36:5-6 NJB).

We have heard so many stories of similar instances, yet
rarely stop to think about the wisdom animals have to detect
a problem and the various ways they use to attempt to communicate with us.

In closing this chapter I would like you to consider the
following as a demonstration of the wisdom of animals.
Then ask yourself which would probably be the more sensi-
ble choice, having a child or a dog as the seeing eyes, protec-
tor, helpmate, and obedient companion for yourself or
someone you love?

A dog trained to be the eyes of a blind person can be
trained with only so much knowledge. Yet that dog will most
probably function far beyond its educational training. This
ability to reason, make decisions, and respond to those decisions is oftentimes incredible. God gave the dog an obedient
nature while a child has a disobedient nature. (There is a
point, however, when a dog can become disobedient to its
owner; that means the situation is not what it should be.)

A friend of mine has a number of blind friends. She
told of one blind friend who worked at a local hospital. Her
seeing-eye dog was always by her side to guide her from

room to room to attend each patient. One day, however, her dog blocked her from going into the room of a gentleman she worked with regularly. All her commands and nudges would not budge the dog. A nurse happened to walk by and noticed the blind social worker and the dog. The nurse told her that the man who had been in the room had passed away that morning. Another situation involved a blind friend who regularly went to her apartment's dumpster to throw her trash away, accompanied by her seeing-eye dog. One evening as they approached the dumpster, the dog suddenly stopped, emitted a low growl, and blocked its master from going forward. She then heard footsteps hurriedly running away.

Some animals possess keen senses, intelligence, reasoning, and spiritual insight that seem to go beyond human awareness and rationale.

Chapter IV

Thankfulness and Praise to God

GREAT is *the Lord, and greatly to be praised in the city of our God,* in *the mountain of his holiness* (Psalm 48:1 KJV).

St. Francis of Assisi (1182-1226), founder of the Franciscan order, taught kindness to animals. He was especially attracted by the meek innocence of his animal friends. Filled with an overflowing love, he called all creatures, however small, his brothers and sisters, for he knew they all had the same origin as himself.

St. Francis noted, "There is no degradation in the dignity of human nature in claiming kinship with creatures so beautiful, so wonderful, who praise God in the forest even as the angels praise Him in heaven."

A Thankful Heart

God provides for and takes care of all His creation. Therefore, all His creation should be thankful and praise Him. God created us all—not because He had to, but because He wanted to. God provided amply for all of us to live an everlasting, glorified life. Animals automatically give thanks and praise to God because their spirits are one with His. Man, however, chooses whether or not he should be grateful to God and praise Him.

In this chapter, Scriptures will illustrate that animals do, indeed, give God thanks and praise Him. I will also share a touching story with you that illustrates what can happen when man interferes with God's plans to care for His creatures.

God Loves Us All

God not only created everything, but He also made plans to care for all He had created. He even cares for creatures as numerous as the sparrows. The Bible says: "Are not two sparrows sold for a farthing? and one of them shall not fall on the ground without your Father" (Matthew 10:29 KJV). As the Book of Jonah tells us, God spoke to Jonah about His concern for man and the cattle with him. It says: "And why shouldn't I feel sorry for a great city like Nineveh with its 120,000 people in utter spiritual darkness, and all its cattle?" (Jonah 4:11 TLB).

God's care for all His creation is spoken of in the Book of Job quite often. It says:

> *For robbers prosper. Go ahead and provoke God—it makes no difference! He will supply your every need anyway! Who doesn't know that the Lord does things like that? Ask the dumbest beast—he knows that it is so; ask the birds—they will tell you; or let the earth teach you, or the fish of the sea. For the soul of every living thing is in the hand of God, and the breath of all mankind* (Job 12:6-10 TLB).

> *Wilt thou hunt the prey for the lion? or fill the appetite of the young lions, When they couch in their dens, and abide in the covert to lie in wait? Who provideth for the raven his food? when his young ones cry unto God, they wander for lack of meat* (Job 38:39-41 KJV).

Matthew Henry makes the explanation of Job 38:39-41 easy to understand. Though man does not provide for the wild animals, God does. God takes care of all His creatures. He writes:

"God provides food for the inferior creatures. 'Let us try that then: *Wilt thou hunt the prey for the lion?* Thou valuest thyself upon thy possessions of cattle which thou wast once owner of, the oxen, the asses, and camels, that were fed at thy crib; but wilt thou undertake the maintenance of the lions, and *the young lions, when they couch in their dens,* waiting for a prey? No, they can shift for themselves without thee: But I do it.' The all-sufficiency of the divine providence has wherewithal to satisfy the desire of every living thing. See the bounty of the divine Providence, that, wherever it has given life, it will give livelihood. The young ravens v. 41, ravenous birds, are fed by the divine Providence. *Who* but God *provides for the raven his food?* They *cry* and this is interpreted a crying to God. It being the cry of nature, it is looked upon as directed to the God of nature. Some way or other he provides for them, so that they grow up, and come to maturity. And he that takes this care of the young ravens certainly will not be wanting to his people."[15]

All Must Praise Him

In return for His care, God expects all His creatures to give Him thanks and to praise Him. God created all His creatures, including mankind, to love Him and to look to Him for all their needs. We cannot imagine the love God has for His creation. The Bible offers many examples of the glory and goodness of God. I would like to share some of them with you, beginning with the Psalms: "Let every thing that hath breath praise the Lord. Praise ye the Lord" (Psalm 150:6 KJV).

Yahweh is generous to all, his tenderness embraces all his creatures. All your creatures shall thank you, Yahweh, and your faithful shall bless you (Psalm 145:9-10 NJB).

All look to you in hope and you feed them with the food of the season. And, with generous hand, you satisfy the desires of every living creature (Psalm 145:15-16 NJB).

*Let everything he has made give praise to him. For he issued
his command, and they came into being; he established them
forever and forever. His orders will never be revoked. And
praise him down here on earth, you creatures of the ocean
depths. Let fire and hail, snow, rain, wind and weather, all
obey. Let the mountains and hills, the fruit trees and cedars,
the wild animals and cattle, the snakes and birds, the kings
and all the people, with their rulers and their judges, young
men and maidens, old men and children–all praise the
Lord together. For he alone is worthy. His glory is far
greater than all of earth and heaven* (Psalm 148:5-13
TLB).

In First Chronicles, David states that all creation is to be
thankful to God for His eternal mercy. *The NIV Matthew
Henry Commentary* (1992), refers this Scripture back to Psalm
96:10-13 (KJV), in which all creation is included in the praise
to God.

*Fear before him, all the earth; the world also shall be stable,
that it be not moved. Let the heavens be glad, and let the
earth rejoice: and let* men *say among the nations, The Lord
reigneth. Let the sea roar, and the fulness thereof: let the
fields rejoice, and all that* is *therein. Then shall the trees of
the wood sing out at the presence of the Lord, because he
cometh to judge the earth. O give thanks unto the Lord; for*
he is *good; for his mercy* endureth *for ever* (I Chronicles
16:30-34 KJV).

*Let the sea roar, and the fulness thereof; the world, and they
that dwell therein. Let the floods clap* their *hands: let the
hills be joyful together Before the Lord; for he cometh to
judge the earth: with righteousness shall he judge the world,
and the people with equity* (Psalm 98:7-9 KJV).

Richard Bauckham, in his book *The Theology of the Book of
Revelation*, explains in Revelation 5:6-13 that first we see the
Lamb, Christ, triumphant over death, standing on the throne,

and the center of worship in Heaven from the living creatures and the elders. Next the angels join in the praise and
worship to the Lamb, then the circle finally expands to include the whole of creation. Both God and Jesus the Lamb
are worshiped together. They are both referred to as the Al-
pha and the Omega, the beginning and the end. Christ is the
agent who can reconcile all creation to Himself.[16]

God asks only for us to obey Him and He will fulfill all
our needs. Jesus Christ is the key to our salvation (and that
of all creation) because man sinned. Man was given dominion over the lower world, which means he must care for
God's lesser creatures. For some creatures man has been a
good caretaker, but for others man has only brought destruction. I speak with some remorse because I was part of
the destruction of God's intended purpose for one of His little creatures. My husband and I had the opportunity to raise
a baby skunk and we simply could not resist it. Stinky, the little skunk, had the best life man could provide for a skunk in
captivity, but it certainly was not the ideal life God intended
for him to have. I know Stinky would have been far more
thankful if we had let him go free, as God created him to be.

Stinky, the Skunk

*When we first married, my husband, a teacher, brought
home a baby skunk that one of his students had found in a barn.
The little guy didn't have his eyes open yet and, by most accounts, didn't have much of a chance of surviving. I was in college at the time, and we spent our weekends with my parents,
who lived on a farm with quite a few cats. Two of the cats were
mothers with new litters of kittens. My parents suggested we
take little Stinky out to see if either one of the mother cats might
nurse him until he was old enough to survive on his own. The
idea worked extremely well. In fact, Stinky became so popular
that both mother cats claimed him.*

*One cat had her litter in the grain shed and the other cat
had her family of kittens in the old barn. One day we would go*

out to find Stinky living with the kittens in the grain shed, and by the afternoon he would be transported by that cat to the old barn. This went on for about two months and it was all we could do to keep up with Stinky. Both mother cats claimed him, as did the kittens, and they all grew up playing with each other. When my husband and I moved the next fall to another town, Stinky went with us. I believe that Stinky had developed a false sense of security because he always expected every cat and dog he met to be friendly with him. Of course, every one of them just sniffed him, turned up its nose and ran away. Stinky wanted so much to have friends, but none of God's little creatures (except for the cats and dogs he grew up with on the farm) would have anything to do with him.

Stinky gave us the knowledge that all animals need love and someone, or something, to cuddle with. He had a little stuffed tiger that went with him everywhere. Stinky also loved making a new home every once in awhile. The first indication would be when he moved his little stuffed tiger. He would build a home under the bed in one bedroom for awhile, then in another bedroom, and then move to a closet. Since the closet doors slid easily, he was able to open them. If any clothes were left lying around, they would end up in his home. Stinky, you see, always wanted a nice soft bed. And, because he could reach the clothes hamper, he had a never-ending supply of bedding.

Most people were somewhat afraid to come into our house while Stinky was a resident. Stinky, however, was initially just as frightened of them as they were of him. Guests could visit all day and never see Stinky, since he would stay hidden. They would, however, hear the hissing sound he made when he was trying to frighten them away. Stinky would hiss, run at our guests, put his tail straight up in the air, and give three forward stomps to indicate his power. Since his scent sac was removed, we didn't have to worry about any aftereffects, thankfully!

At night things would, upon occasion, get pretty wild. Since skunks are nocturnal, Stinky would want to play after the family had gone to bed. In the middle of the night we could hear

Stinky running around, stomping, hissing, and building a new home. Although he sometimes kept us awake, he was a great deal of fun.

If Stinky had made a decision about joining a Christian faith, I believe he would have chosen Catholicism because whenever he would get out, he headed straight for the local Catholic church. Stinky had the best life possible for a domesticated skunk, but he should have lived out in the woods with his brothers and sisters where God intended him to be. We could not, however, let him go after he had been taken from his natural home. Still, Stinky loved the outdoors, so we built him a big fenced-in area under the house. So he would not dig out, we put the wire down under the ground and covered it with dirt, and closed him in with a wire gate. But one night, Stinky disappeared. The door was left open, so we knew he hadn't gotten out on his own. We never knew exactly what happened to him. We have always felt sorrow and pain for whatever Stinky may have had to suffer after his disappearance.

God feels pain when His creatures are abused. My guilt of not taking more precautions to protect Stinky left me with a feeling of failure, and pain for my loss. Stinky trusted our family and looked to us for his complete care. I am so thankful that the Psalmist revealed that my loss, and what I considered to be Stinky's loss, will be turned into glory.

So let's conclude this chapter with a Scripture that restates and attests to the praise and recognition our Lord will receive from all creation when Jesus returns. The Book of Romans says: "For of him, and through him, and to him, *are* all things: to whom *be* glory for ever. Amen" (Romans 11:36 KJV).

Psalm 103:22 says all His works will praise Him. All creation, angels, man, and the lesser animals will praise Him. Although we do not see how the animals praise God, we do not understand all the things of nature, either. The Psalms say: "Bless the Lord, all his works in all places of his dominion: bless the Lord, O my soul" (Psalm 103:22 KJV). "According to thy name, O God, so *is* thy praise unto the ends of the earth: thy right hand is full of righteousness" (Psalm 48:10 KJV).

Chapter V

Sinlessness, Sacrifice, and Forgiveness

For every beast of the forest is *mine,* and *the cattle upon a thousand hills. I know all the fowls of the mountains: and the wild beasts of the field* are *mine"* (Psalm 50:10-11 KJV).

Why Animal Sacrifices?

When I started researching *Will I See Fido in Heaven?*, I really did not give much thought to the sinlessness of animals. Romans 8:20 states that they are sinless, but I did not expect other Scriptures to indicate the same. I did, however, wonder why the Jews sacrificed animals to make themselves righteous for eternal life. Until I read First Peter 1:19 where it compares Jesus to the innocence of a lamb, I did not understand the purpose of Old Testament animal sacrifices. We know that because of man's cruelty, many animals have been tortured and killed. Since man has dominion over the animals, they are completely helpless against him. It helps to ease our pain, however, if we keep in mind that God knew how cruel man would be to His lesser creatures, and that He planned for the time when they would not have to suffer in pain and death but would be renewed for eternal life with Him in His new Heaven and earth. In this chapter, I will use Scripture to explain why the sinless are sacrificed to make atonement for man's sins, and include a story about a wren family that made a tremendous sacrifice, along with a story about a "wrong-way" turtle.

Animals Are Innocent

Both Romans 8:20 and First Peter 1:19 speak of the sinlessness and innocence of the animals. Peter says: "But with the precious blood of Christ, as of a lamb without blemish and without spot" (I Peter 1:19 KJV). So, too, the Book of Wisdom states that the innocent or righteous of the world (which includes elect angels, followers of God, and the lesser creatures) will have immortal life with God. It says:

> *For God did not make Death, he takes no pleasure in destroying the living. To exist—for this he created all things; the creatures of the world have health in them, in them is no fatal poison, and Hades has no power over the world: for uprightness is immortal. But the godless call for Death with deed and word, counting him friend, they wear themselves out for him; with him they make a pact, worthy as they are to belong to him* (Wisdom 1:13-16 NJB).

The lesser animals were put under the curse of sin because of the sins of man. Yet, they are sinless. The Book of Romans says: "For the creature was made subject to vanity, not willingly, but by reason of him who hath subjected *the same* in hope" (Romans 8:20 KJV). Matthew 10:16 (NIV) says: "I am sending you out like sheep among wolves. Therefore be as shrewd as snakes and as innocent as doves." Innocent means blameless, knowing no evil, free from guilt or wrongdoing.

Sacrificial Animals

During the time of the Old Testament, the priests always had to enter the outer court (tent) of the tabernacle to perform their ritual duties in order to sanctify their people. Once each year, the high priest went into the inner court, into the Holy of Holies, with the blood of an animal. After

Adam sinned in the Garden, man needed animal sacrifices to cover his fleshy sins until God sent the Messiah to die once and for all to redeem man's soul. The Bible says: "And unto the children of Israel thou shalt speak, saying, Take ye a kid of the goats for a sin offering; and a calf and a lamb, *both* of the first year, without blemish, for a burnt offering" (Leviticus 9:3 KJV).

Every year on the Day of Atonement, the Jews would bring a bull and two he-goats for sacrifice. The priests would kill a bull and bring its blood to the Holy of Holies, the sacred place where God's presence prevailed. The blood of the bull was sprinkled on the mercy seat in the temple. Lots were cast for the two goats. One would be used as a sin sacrifice, its blood also being sprinkled on the mercy seat; the other as a live scapegoat. The priests would lay their hands on the head of the scapegoat, and put all the sins of the people on its head. After their prayer, the goat was taken to the desert and released. (See Leviticus 16:5-28 KJV.) This sacrifice allowed for the covering, or probation, of sin for the people for one year. Lewis B. Smedes,[17] author and retired professor from Fuller Theological Seminary, explained this practice to me. He said; "God took a bundle of human sins off a man's back and tied it to a goat. He took the goat out into a solitary place, sins and all—a scapegoat—leaving the sinner free of his burden."

Man still tries to use the scapegoat form of self-atonement. Just as Adam blamed Eve, and she blamed the snake, we attempt to lay our sins on our parents, God, our spouse, or our children. Scapegoats (people held captive for crimes committed by others) can be found imprisoned all over the world.

Jesus as the Lamb
The Bible often compares Jesus to a lamb. What does Jesus, as the slain Lamb of God, symbolize? Let's look at the Scriptures and compare the sacrificial animals to Jesus. I do

want to add here that in no way is this book implying that animals are as valued or as sacred as the precious blood of Jesus. However, there is a very specific reason why animals were used as sacrifices for the sins of man until Jesus came. While man was riddled with guilt and sin, animals were sinless. Sacrificial animals were especially pure, since they ate only vegetation. They were free of the parasites and disease that the meat-eating unclean animals were subject to. After all, the purpose for those scavenger animals was to eat all decayed dead flesh to keep disease down. Clean animals were domestic animals that were worth a great deal of money to their owners.

Jesus was referred to as a lamb because lambs were considered to be without spots or blemishes. To better understand this definition, let's look at what the words *spot* and *blemish* mean. The word *spotless* means "pure, undefiled, immaculate." Without *blemish* means physically perfect. Sacrificial animals could not be sick, injured, or have any physical defects. Even an animal taken from the household of a non-Jew was considered mutilated and physically imperfect. Jesus, like a lamb, was perfect in every way. Peter says: "but with the precious blood of Christ, like that of a lamb without blemish or spot" (1 Peter 1:19 RSV).

Jesus came to deliver a new message and establish a new covenant between God and man. He came to replace sacrifice with compassion. After Jesus' death and resurrection, animal sacrifices were no longer needed. The shedding of the blood of an animal no longer covered sins. Jesus was the perfect sacrifice; He was without blemish. He was much higher than animals, and more than just a normal man. He was the Son of God. He was a life-giving Spirit to all who would receive Him. Jesus was not born of an imperfect world, but was conceived by the Holy Spirit. Instead of a one-year probation from sin through animal sacrifice, Jesus offered a complete and permanent pardon from sin to all who would accept His sacrifice. The Bible says:

But when Christ appeared as a high priest of the good things that have come, then through the greater and more perfect tent (not made with hands, that is, not of this creation) he entered once for all into the Holy Place, taking not the blood of goats and calves but his own blood, thus securing an eternal redemption. For if the sprinkling of defiled persons with the blood of goats and bulls and with the ashes of a heifer sanctifies for the purification of the flesh, how much more shall the blood of Christ, who through the eternal Spirit offered himself without blemish to God, purify your conscience from dead works to serve the living God (Hebrews 9:11-14 RSV).

Isaiah 53:6-7 (KJV), refers to Jesus, the coming Messiah. Even though He was innocent, Jesus would not speak in His own defense. Therefore, He was killed just as the sheep that cannot speak in their own defense are sent to slaughter. God put all the sins of the world on Jesus. Sinful man required the ultimate scapegoat: God offered Jesus to carry the sins of the world into the God-forsaken desert of hell. The Bible says:

All we like sheep have gone astray; we have turned every one to his own way; and the Lord hath laid on him the iniquity of us all. He was oppressed, and he was afflicted, yet he opened not his mouth: he is brought as a lamb to the slaughter, and as a sheep before her shearers is dumb, so he openeth not his mouth (Isaiah 53:6-7 KJV).

The Scriptures repeatedly say that God took no pleasure in the animals sacrificed by the Jews. Nor did He take pleasure in the suffering Jesus endured for man's sins. By physically sacrificing the sinless, God could save all sinners by cleansing them of their sins. Eternity will have no more death, pain, or suffering for all of God's creatures that worship Him.

The following story is about two little innocent baby
wrens that were rescued from death by adoptive parent
wrens. The story illustrates that animals are capable of great
sacrifice. The adult birds offered a sacrifice of love and hard
work to feed and care for the little ones.

The Wren Family

*My cousin, Marilyn, lives on a farm near a small town in
northwest Missouri. She and her husband, Bob, enjoy sitting
outside and watching the beautiful creatures God has made.
Several years ago, Marilyn became concerned about one little
family of wrens. These birds had built a home in a hollowed-out
gourd birdhouse that was on a pole, one onto which a cat could
easily crawl. One of the old cats discovered the bird's nest on the
pole and tried several times to catch the mother.*

*One day, as Marilyn and her husband were sitting outside
in the morning having coffee and preparing for the day, they
noticed that the baby wrens were crying at the top of their lungs
and the mother was nowhere to be found. After a few hours,
Marilyn decided the mother must have been caught by the old
cat. Since she had noticed another family of wrens nearby that
were still waiting for their new babies to hatch, she decided that
she'd try to save the little orphaned wrens by moving their
gourd birdhouse right under the expectant parents' birdhouse
in the nearby tree.*

*Marilyn hung the gourd birdhouse and waited to see what
would happen. The babies continued to cry at the top of their
lungs. Within a short while, the adult wrens flew away and
came back with food for the little wrens that had lost their
mother. The adults knew the babies could not take care of themselves and raised the newly-adopted babies as their own.*

The sacrifice the birds made was certainly more than
many humans would make. Getting worms and other food
for the baby birds was a constant and ongoing process. It
was work much harder than most of us would care to commit ourselves.

Thousands and thousands of men and women have given their lives to protect our country and the freedom we have to worship God. We love our children, and we sacrifice for their daily needs. Some people have sacrificed all the material goods they had in order to save the life of a family member. Many of us also make sacrifices for the well-being of our animals. Some of us have risked our lives to save our pets. Certainly, many animals have sacrificed their own lives to save their masters.

Because of Jesus, we can be forgiven our sins and rewarded for our sacrifices if we place our faith and trust in Him. The animals will be rewarded as well. The Crucifixion of Christ was God's final and most memorable act of compassion. The Book of John says: "I am the good shepherd: the good shepherd giveth his life for the sheep" (John 10:11 KJV). God wants us to know that the debts for all our sins (both those we have committed and those we ever will commit) have already been paid by the blood that was shed by our Lord and Savior, Jesus Christ.

I wonder if the rest of creation knows something that mankind finds difficult to accept? Revelation 5:13 speaks of every creature—man, angels, and the lesser animals—as recognizing Jesus as the Savior of the world. All creatures, in fact, seem to understand what Jesus did for man as the sacrificial lamb. All, that is, except man.

> *And every creature which is in heaven, and on the earth, and under the earth, and such as are in the sea, and all that are in them, heard I saying, Blessing, and honour, and glory, and power, be unto him that sitteth upon the throne, and unto the Lamb for ever and ever* (Revelation 5:13 KJV).

From time to time people will make sacrifices for others and for God's lesser creatures. Included in these sacrifices are efforts made to help animals left baffled and confused after their natural terrain has been destroyed to make highways and other man-made conveniences. My husband, Ron, always tries to do his part for the unprotected. Once he even tried to save a turtle that was in great peril.

Wrong-Way Turtle

Ron came bounding into the house one evening and said, "Mary, you really would have been proud of me today. I stopped and saved a turtle that was right in the middle of the highway from certain death."

Now let's look for a moment at the situation through the eyes of a man who loves all God's little creatures. Here was this little box turtle cruising across the highway, pouring on the gas at top turtle power. Only divine or human intervention could save the little critter from grievous bodily harm. Deciding that human intervention might be the best answer in this case, Ron took action. He went on to tell his story: "I saw the turtle, pulled the car over to the side of the road, backed up and got out, went out to the middle of the highway, and brought the turtle back to the side of the highway so it would not be run over." Then, he paused for a moment and said, "Well, I am not so sure I did the right thing after all. You see, the turtle was heading to the west side of the highway and I put it back on the east side." We contemplated the possible outcomes and prayed for divine intervention to take over in case the little turtle would try to cross the highway again. If another well-meaning member of the human species felt the need to be a "Good Samaritan" and stopped to help "Wrong-Way," we hoped the rescuer would be more in tune with the little fellow's future plans than Ron was.

I suppose the moral of this story would be: "If you want to save the life of another, make sure you point them in the right direction."

I experience sacrifice every time I come home. I am greeted by wagging tails, barking voices, and puppy kisses exhibiting pure, sincere love. Their affections are a sacrifice of praise to me for caring for them. You see, the act of sacrifice is the ultimate expression of love. It involves the giving of ourselves in humility and joy. Our dogs always give us an offering of praise every time we come home.

Chapter VI

The Fall and Rise of Creation

For all creatures, human and animal—and seven times more for sinners—there is death and blood and strife and the sword, disasters, famine, affliction, plague. These things were all created for the wicked, and the Flood came because of them (Sirach 40:8-10 NJB).

Behold the fowls of the air: for they sow not, neither do they reap, nor gather into barns; yet your heavenly Father feedeth them... (Matthew 6:26 KJV).

God's Plan

Will I See Fido in Heaven? has addressed the fall of mankind into sin and how man's sins affected the animals. We have also discussed how God has made provisions to rescue all His creatures from their suffering so they can live with Him through all eternity, by sending His Son to die for us. Now let us go back in history to the time when the world first began in such beauty and innocence, then to the fall of man into sin, when corrosion and death came into the world. Then, we will look at God's promise of a new Heaven and a new earth, where all who worship Him will be renewed to live in eternal joy and peace.

The Garden of Eden

In the beginning, God created a perfect world. He created angels, man, animals, and a beautiful universe. God created man in His own image with his own free will to choose good from evil. God did not give the lesser animals this free will. As we said earlier, the free will given to man is a distinct factor that separates us from the lesser creatures. Man could choose good or evil. That doesn't seem like a difficult decision to make, but just stop and think how often we make selfish choices. Man also had an adversary to deal with: Satan. Satan, formerly known as Lucifer, wanted revenge because God kicked him and his demonic band of angels out of Heaven. The story of the fall of man in Genesis 3:1-15 reveals how man's disobedience turned God's creation into the mess it is today.

In the Garden, life was good. There was no sin, and Adam and Eve lived like a king and queen. They didn't have to go shopping for clothes. The animals, too, had a good life. They could walk around without the fear of being some other creature's main course. All lived in the beautiful Garden of Eden in perfect peace and harmony. The Book of Genesis says:

> *And the Lord God took the man, and put him into the garden of Eden to dress it and to keep it. And the Lord God commanded the man, saying, Of every tree of the garden thou mayest freely eat: But of the tree of the knowledge of good and evil, thou shalt not eat of it: for in the day that thou eatest thereof thou shalt surely die* (Genesis 2:15-17 KJV).

Adam and Eve did not wear clothes, as all flesh was innocent. The Book of Genesis says that man was not embarrassed about being naked: "Now although the man and his wife were both naked, neither of them was embarrassed or ashamed" (Genesis 2:25 TLB).

It didn't take long, though, for man to sin and bring death on all God's creatures. Satan deceived the woman, and our first parents sinned. Satan got Adam and Eve to eat fruit from the tree of the knowledge of good and evil (KJV). Satan, a spirit being, needed to use a body of flesh to do his dirty work. Since the serpent was the most crafty of all the creatures God had made, Satan decided to use the snake to talk Eve into eating the fruit. Man had authority over the animals, and he had authority over Satan, so he could have said, "Satan, you must leave this earth and never return in the name of God." In such a case, Satan would have had to obey. Instead, man chose to eat of the tree and willfully brought mortality on himself and all God's creatures.

Satan first convinced Eve to eat the fruit. Adam joined her in disobeying God's command—and that did it. The Book of Genesis says:

The serpent was the craftiest of all the creatures the Lord God had made. So the serpent came to the woman. "Really?" he asked. "None of the fruit in the garden? God says you mustn't eat any of it?" "Of course we may eat it," the woman told him. "It's only the fruit from the tree at the cen-ter of the garden that we are not to eat. God says we mustn't eat it or even touch it, or we will die." "That's a lie!" the ser-pent hissed. "You'll not die! God knows very well that the instant you eat it you will become like him, for your eyes will be opened—you will be able to distinguish good from evil!" The woman was convinced. How lovely and fresh looking it was! And it would make her so wise! So she ate some of the fruit and gave some to her husband, and he ate it too (Genesis 3:1-6 TLB).

Adam and Eve were foolish to believe Satan's lies. After they ate the fruit, they became ashamed of their bodies (aware of their sins). Animals do not know of sin. They do not wear clothes and they are not ashamed of their "naked-ness." Man's only responsibility was to care for God's garden. After partaking of the fruit, however, man had to work for a living. For this reason, he recruited many of God's other creatures to be either his slaves or his victims. Everything now had to die. The serpent was singled out from all animals to be cursed. The snake had to crawl on its belly and be despised by both man and animals all the days of its life. It's interesting to note that Satan, the prince of darkness, would use a creature that now lives in darkness to tempt mankind. Because man sinned, all God's creation has to suffer in sickness and physical death. The Book of Genesis explains how the serpent was also punished because of Satan:

> And as they ate it, suddenly they became aware of their na-
> kedness, and were embarrassed. So they strung fig leaves to-
> gether to cover themselves around the hips. That evening
> they heard the sound of the Lord God walking in the gar-
> den; and they hid themselves among the trees. The Lord
> God called to Adam, "Why are you hiding?" And Adam re-
> plied, "I heard you coming and didn't want you to see me
> naked. So I hid." "Who told you you were naked?" the Lord
> God asked. "Have you eaten fruit from the tree I warned
> you about?" "Yes," Adam admitted, "but it was the woman
> you gave me who brought me some, and I ate it." Then the
> Lord God asked the woman, "How could you do such a
> thing?" "The serpent tricked me," she replied. So the Lord
> God said to the serpent, "This is your punishment: You are
> singled out from among all the domestic and wild animals
> of the whole earth—to be cursed. You shall grovel in the dust
> as long as you live, crawling along on your belly. From now
> on you and the woman will be enemies, as will all of your
> offspring and hers..." (Genesis 3:7-15 TLB).

As soon as Adam sinned, Satan took control of the earth. Satan wanted to destroy all creation and, through sinful man, could cause endless suffering to God's lesser creatures. God sent Jesus to take the earth back from Satan. Although Satan sometimes uses animals, because they are under the dominion of man, they are not subject to eternal damnation.

In examining these issues, we also have the evidence of physical death. God killed the first animal (the first blood sacrifice) right before the eyes of Adam and Eve and clothed them in animal skins to cover their sin. Fig leaves would not cover their nakedness (sin); only innocent blood could do that. Through the disobedience of Adam and Eve, sin entered the world and death happened. (See Genesis 3:21 TLB.)

After man disobeyed God and fell into sin, God had to keep man from living forever in his physical state. God could not allow His creation to be forever corrupted, so man was banished from the Garden of Eden and the Tree of Life. (See Genesis 3:22-23 TLB.)

Sin continued and the condition of the earth worsened. God decided to destroy both man and animals. God sorrowed over the wickedness of the world. The Book of Genesis says: "And he said, 'I will blot out from the face of the earth all mankind that I created. Yes, and the animals too, and the reptiles and the birds. For I am sorry I made them' " (Genesis 6:7 TLB).

Noah's Ark

God decided to destroy the world with a flood. However, He found one man named Noah who, along with his family, was righteous before Him. God decided to save Noah and his family and at least one pair of each kind of animal. Noah built an ark according to God's instructions and the animals went into the boat. They all remained in the big floating box (ark) for 375 days. After the occupants of the ark disembarked on dry land, God told Noah to make a burnt sacrifice to Him. There were seven pairs of each of the clean animals that were designated to be sacrificial animals.

God, at that point, made a covenant with Noah and the animals that He would never again destroy the earth with water as long as it remained. Genesis 9:8-17 gives us seven accounts of God's covenant with both man and animals concerning our survival on planet Earth as long as the earth remains. It says:

*And God spake unto Noah (Noe), and to his sons with him,
saying, And I, behold, I established my covenant with you,
and with your seed after you;*

*1.   And with every living soul that is with you, as well in all
birds as in cattle and beasts of the earth, that are come forth
out of the ark, and in all the beasts of the earth.*

*2.   I will establish my covenant with you, and all flesh shall
be no more destroyed with the waters of a flood, neither shall
there be from henceforth a flood to waste the earth.*

*3.   And God said: This is the sign of the covenant which I
give between me and you, and to every living soul that is with
you, for perpetual generations.*

*4.   I will set my bow in the clouds, and it shall be the sign of
a covenant between me, and between the earth.*

*5.   And when I shall cover the sky with clouds, my bow shall
appear in the clouds: And I will remember my covenant with
you, and with every living soul that beareth flesh: and there
shall no more be waters of a flood to destroy all flesh.*

*6.   And the bow shall be in the clouds, and I shall see it, and
shall remember the everlasting covenant, that was made between God and every living soul of all flesh which is upon the
earth.*

*7.   And God said to Noe: This shall be the sign of the cov-
enant which I have established between me and all flesh upon
the earth.*   **DOUAY-RHEIMS Bible Genesis 9:9-17.**

At that point, God put fear of man into the hearts of the
animals. God stated that all animals are to become food for
man. In fact, they then became food for each other. The Bible says:

*And God blessed Noah and his sons, and said unto them,
Be fruitful, and multiply, and replenish the earth. And the
fear of you and the dread of you shall be upon every beast of*

the earth, and upon every fowl of the air, upon all that moveth upon *the earth, and upon all the fishes of the sea; into your hand are they delivered. Every moving thing that liveth shall be meat for you; even as the green herb have I given you all things* (Genesis 9:1-3 KJV).

The Scriptures do not refer to animals as sinful. Rather, the Bible speaks of sinful man and the fallen angels as evil. Second Peter 2:9-12 (KJV) speaks symbolically of godless men as natural brute beasts. When the Scriptures speak of these brute beasts, it is important to realize that the Word is comparing us to the altered nature of animals in this world. Brute beasts (mankind) are also mentioned in Jude 10 as the ones who will be destroyed by their own corruption.

The Lord knoweth how to deliver the godly out of temptations, and to reserve the unjust unto the day of judgment to be punished: ... Whereas angels, which are greater in power and might, bring not railing accusation against them before the Lord. But these, as natural brute beasts, made to be taken and destroyed, speak evil of the things that they understand not; and shall utterly perish in their own corruption (II Peter 2:9,11-12 KJV).

For the creature was made subject to vanity, not willingly, but by reason of him who hath subjected the same *in hope* (Romans 8:20 KJV).

Eternity

Though all creatures are subject to man's cruelty, God loves all His creation and has made plans for all His children and the lesser creatures to enjoy His eternal Kingdom. (See Psalm 145:9-10,13,15-21 AMP.)

The Lord is good to all and His tender mercies are over all His creatures. God is merciful in all His works (actions, transactions, activities). He cannot lie. His promise is for eternity. For all the torture and abuse that many of the innocent animals suffered throughout God's earth, they will be rewarded in Heaven with eternal bliss. Jesus is over all things created. He is the supreme being. He is the Savior. He is the begotten. He Himself is over all creation and He produced and can reconcile creation back to Himself. *Prototokos* means first born or first begotten. In His relationship to the Father, it is in His priority to and His preeminence over creation; not in the sense of being the first to be born. Christ holds the same relation to all creation as God the Father; He is above all creation. God will have all His creation by His side. The Bible says:

> *Who is the image of the invisible God, the firstborn of every creature: For by him were all things created, that are in heaven, and that are in the earth, visible and invisible, whether* they be *thrones, or dominions, or principalities, or powers: all things were created by him, and for him: And he is before all things, and by him all things consist. And he is the head of the body, the church: who is the beginning, the firstborn from the dead; that in all* things *he might have the preeminence. For it pleased* the Father *that in him should all fulness dwell; And, having made peace through the blood of his cross, by him to reconcile all things unto himself; by him,* I say, *whether* they be *things in earth, or things in heaven* (Colossians 1:15-20 KJV).

In the Book of Revelation, God shows John a vision of what will happen in the future. This vision refers not only to man, but also to animals. These verses include both symbols and real forms of life that God created to tell us what is yet to come. The number "four" possibly stands for the created universe; thus, the four living creatures represent all creation.

A more extensive explanation is given in the New International Student Edition of the Bible. The Lamb is Jesus and the angels are the created angels of God. The creatures are all God's creatures who live in, on, and above the earth, in the sea, and in the heavens. The Book of Revelation says:

> *Then I saw a Lamb, looking as if it had been slain, standing in the center of the throne, encircled by the four living*

creatures and the elders. He had seven horns and seven eyes, which are the seven spirits of God sent out into all the earth. He came and took the scroll from the right hand of him who sat on the throne. And when he had taken it, the four living creatures and the twenty-four elders fell down before the Lamb. Each one had a harp and they were holding golden bowls full of incense, which are the prayers of the saints. And they sang a new song: "You are worthy to take the scroll and to open its seals, because you were slain, and with your blood you purchased men for God from every tribe and language and people and nation. You have made them to be a kingdom and priests to serve our God, and they will reign on the earth." Then I looked and heard the voice of many angels, numbering thousands upon thousands, and ten thousand times ten thousand. They encircled the throne and the living creatures and the elders. In a loud voice they sang: "Worthy is the Lamb, who was slain, to receive power and wealth and wisdom and strength and honor and glory and praise!" Then I heard every creature in heaven and on earth and under the earth and on the sea, and all that is in them, singing: "To him who sits on the throne and to the Lamb be praise and honor and glory and power, for ever and ever!" The four living creatures said, "Amen," and the elders fell down and worshiped (Revelation 5:6-14 NIV).

Read Isaiah 11:6-9 in the King James Version of the Bible and follow your reading with *Matthew Henry's Commentary* on these verses. Matthew Henry explains how God uses the dispositions of animals to illustrate to us what Heaven will be like for us and, at the same time, what life will be like for the animal kingdom. We can believe that our eternal home will be much like the Garden of Eden before Adam and Eve sinned, when all creatures lived together in harmony and love. Possibly, like the serpent and Balaam's donkey, all creation will one day be able to communicate with each other in total understanding.

Read Genesis 11:1-9 of the King James Version. God certainly has the power to make all mankind communicate together again—so why not the animals? It was through the tongue that sin entered the world and the tongue still continues to cause destruction. It may be that God had a very good reason for not wanting the animals to speak with man in this sinful world. The Book of Isaiah says:

> *The wolf also shall dwell with the lamb, and the leopard shall lie down with the kid; and the calf and the young lion and the fatling together; and a little child shall lead them. And the cow and the bear shall feed; their young ones shall lie down together: and the lion shall eat straw like the ox. And the sucking child shall play on the hole of the asp, and the weaned child shall put his hand on the cockatrice' den. They shall not hurt nor destroy in all my holy mountain: for the earth shall be full of the knowledge of the Lord, as the waters cover the sea* (Isaiah 11:6-9 KJV).

The following is from *Matthew Henry's Commentary* on this passage:

> "Unity or concord, intimated in these figurative promises, that even *the wolf shall dwell* peaceably *with the lamb*; men of the most fierce and furious dispositions shall have their temper so strangely altered by the grace of Christ that they shall live in love even with the weakest and such as formerly were an easy prey. Christ, who is our peace, came to slay all enmities and to settle lasting friendships among his followers, particularly between Jews and Gentiles. *The leopard shall* not only not tear the kid, but shall *lie down with her*: even *their young ones shall lie down together*, and shall be trained up in blessed amity. *The lion* shall cease to be ravenous and *shall eat straw like the ox*, as some think all the beasts of prey did before the fall. *The asp* and *the cockatrice* shall cease to be venomous, so that parents shall let their children *play* with them."[18]

An attorney with whom I'm acquainted reads the Bible every day. One morning several years ago as he was reading in Isaiah 11:6-9 he became aware of the reference to a time to come when the world will have eternal peace and the wolf shall lie down with the lamb. He reads the Bible through each year faithfully, but this was the first time he had really been made aware of what that Scripture was saying. He had a dog named Zack that was about 14 years old, and they had been great friends for many years. That same day while at his office he received a frantic call from his wife saying their dog was stumbling around in the yard and could hardly stand up. He told her to take him to the vet. Before he could get home, his wife called to say that Zack had died at the vet's office. On his way home he said, "Lord, I would like to have Zack with me in Heaven." At that moment the Lord spoke to him saying, "Remember the Scripture you read this morning?" The attorney thought for a minute, *What Scripture?* As soon as he arrived at home he opened his Bible to where he had been reading and read again Isaiah 11:6-9. Peace and joy came flooding over him and the divine assurance came that one day he will again be with his old pal for all eternity. "The wolf also shall dwell with the lamb." All will be at peace on God's holy mountain.

Martin Luther (1483-1546), a German priest, was the religious reformer who led the Protestant Reformation in Germany. In his speaking on Deuteronomy 22:6, which forbids the harming of the mother bird if her eggs or chicks are gathered up, Luther wrote: "What else does this law teach but that by the kind treatment of animals they are to learn gentleness and kindness."

> *If a bird's nest chance to be before thee in the way in any tree, or on the ground,* whether they be *young ones, or eggs, and the dam sitting upon the young, or upon the eggs, thou shalt not take the dam with the young* (Deuteronomy 22:6 KJV).

Dix Harwood, author of *Love for Animals*, self-published in 1928, tells the story of a grieving little girl being comforted by Luther, who assured her that her pet dog that had died would surely go to Heaven. Luther is said to have told her that in the "new heavens and new earth...all creatures will not only be harmless, but lovely and joyful." Luther quoted the following scripture:

> *And God shall wipe away all tears from their eyes; and there shall be no more death, neither sorrow, nor crying, neither shall there be any more pain: for the former things are passed away* (Revelation 21:4 KJV).

> *He that overcometh shall inherit all things; and I will be his God, and he shall be my son* (Revelation 21:7 KJV).

Chapter VII

The True Message

For the earnest expectation of the creature waiteth for the manifestation of the sons of God (Romans 8:19 KJV).

An Important Lesson

When I was about six years old, I announced one Sunday that I did not want to go to church. My father, a wonderful Christian who understood the importance of hearing God's Word, said, "Well, Mary Catherine, if you don't go to church you might not go to Heaven." (No, dad did not really mean that not going to church would keep me from Heaven, but he knew that worshiping in the house of God was very important.)

I thought for a minute about Heaven and my dog, Tipsy. I certainly did not want to go to Heaven without Tipsy, so I said, "Well, Daddy, if I go to church, then Tipsy has to go too, so we can both go to Heaven." Tipsy did, indeed, go to church with us that morning, and many times after that. Tipsy was tied to the rail right outside the big door that opened into the sanctuary of our little Methodist church in the country. We left the door slightly ajar so she could hear all the sermons.

How I thank God for such loving parents who would put up with a small child's concern for her pet, and for the members of the little church who tolerated this unusual member of their congregation.

God's Plan for the Animals

When Mary went to Bethlehem to give birth to Jesus, she probably rode on a donkey, a sinless beast of burden. When she gave birth, it was in a stable where the servant animals of man were housed. Some of these animals probably witnessed Jesus' birth. They may have even recognized the angels guarding Jesus, just as Balaam's donkey recognized the angel of the Lord.

Jesus, on His final trip to Jerusalem just before His crucifixion, rode on the back of a lowly, sinless donkey. When Jesus returns, He will be riding a white horse out of Heaven—a pure, stately white horse, the most prized of all creatures, the emblem of justice and holiness (Revelation 19:11 TLB). He will redeem the bodies of the animals and make them perfect, just as He will ours. All His creation will be made perfect for eternal life with God. Jesus entered the world as an innocent lamb. He will return as the Lion of the tribe of Juda. (See Revelation 5:5 KJV.)

The Scriptures tell us that animals do have an eternal existence with God, along with the children of God. They have a soul and spirit, as we do. They are sinless creatures, and they recognize Jesus as Savior of the world. All animals are to praise God and look to Him for their needs.

Paul's Epistle to the Ephesians tells us that God works all things (creation) after His will. (See Ephesians 1:1.) Christians inherit the Kingdom of God as joint heirs with Christ.

The animals also are predestined to receive God's eternal Kingdom of peace and joy. (See Ephesians 1:11 KJV.)

In whom also we have obtained an inheritance, being predestinated according to the purpose of him who worketh all things after the counsel of his own will (Ephesians 1:11 KJV).

Let everything he has made give praise to him. For he issued his command, and they came into being; he established them forever and forever. His orders will never be revoked (Psalm 148:5-6 TLB).

Who shall change our vile body, that it may be fashioned like unto his glorious body, according to the working whereby he is able even to subdue all things unto himself (Philippians 3:21 KJV).

Paul points out in Philippians 3:21 that Jesus is able to change the vile, evil, corrupt bodies of man into glorified perfect bodies like His own, through His own work on the cross, just as He is able to subdue all things (creation) to Himself.

Then Ezra prayed, "You alone are God. You have made the skies and the heavens, the earth and the seas, and everything in them. You preserve it all; and all the angels of heaven worship you (Nehemiah 9:6 TLB).

It seems selfish that we of the human race think that of all creation, we should be the only creatures of any eternal importance. We hardly even recognize the work of angels on our behalf or understand that they are much more knowledgeable than we. The elect angels are always obedient to God.

We know God has a wonderful new Heaven and earth waiting for us, and that He has included all our pets and animals, which He has made. God created the world for an eternal, non-temporal, spiritual existence where body, soul, and spirit are united with God's Spirit. The Garden of Eden seemed to be an eternal existence of perfection for all the creatures God made. Man was given the privilege and responsibility to rule and care for the earth. Yet man ordered his own destruction, and that of the entire physical creation, by accepting Satan and rejecting God. Therefore, both man and animals were thrust into a finite world ruled by guilt, fear, anger, and death.

The spirits of the animals remained connected with God, though, allowing them to see beyond the temporal state, which they were forced to live in because of man's sin. Man, however, became trapped in the temporal state of this life because of his spiritual separation from God. God spoke to man and called him to repent and return to Him. He sent prophets to foretell the future for man if he did not repent, and God allowed the sacrifice of sinless animals to cover man's sins. Finally, He sent His only Son, Jesus Christ, to be crucified to pay the final price for all who would accept His ultimate gift. God has done all this to reconcile man back to an eternal union with Him and the rest of His creation.

Now the lesser animals must wait on the sons of God to be reconciled to God, through Jesus, for their physical renewal in God's eternal Kingdom. Read Romans 8:16-23 again. Then read this:

> *Therefore, if anyone is in Christ, he is a new creation; the old has gone, the new has come! All this is from God, who reconciled us to himself through Christ and gave us the ministry of reconciliation: that God was reconciling the world to himself in Christ, not counting men's sins against them. And he has committed to us the message of reconciliation* (2 Corinthians 5:17-19 NIV).

Through the Tears

I have one final story about Duffy, my beagle. Duffy was 17 years old when he died. Romans 8:19-21 (AMP) has been a comfort to me since he went to Heaven. The two of us went through so much together. My sons grew up, went off to college, and got married, but Duffy and I remained together. We shared the good times and the bad times. But on October 19, 1993, I knew Duffy was in extreme pain and could barely walk and breathe. He had been failing for about six months. Dr. Steinberg, Duffy's veterinarian, told me that I should not let him suffer.

Many times throughout his illness, I had prayed him back to health. But this time I knew I had to let go; it was time. My son, Roman, picked him up and took him to Dr. Steinberg's office.

He was with him until his spirit slipped into his eternal heavenly home. I will always be thankful to my son. I should have gone with him, but I was hurting so badly that I couldn't face the responsibility.

My husband and Roman dug a little grave on the hillside overlooking a beautiful pond that a friend of mine owns, and Duffy's worn-out body was laid to rest until the time when he will get his new one. Though it was a painful decision, I know we were being merciful to Duffy, as God commands us to be. Someday we will all be together again and I will forever be able to be with my family and the creatures God gave me to love on this earth.

The Bible says:

For (even the whole) creation (all nature) waits expectantly and longs earnestly for God's sons to be made known—waits for the revealing, the disclosing of their sonship. For the creation (nature) was subjected to frailty—to futility, condemned to frustration—not because of some intentional fault on its part, but by the will of Him Who so subjected it. [Yet] with the hope that nature (creation) itself will be set free from its bondage to decay and corruption [and gain an entrance] into the glorious freedom of God's children (Romans 8:19-21 AMP).

There are many, many accounts of animals that have demonstrated spiritual knowledge and understanding beyond what the natural man can comprehend. It is truly awe-inspiring to get a glimpse of God's wisdom and the magnificence in which He created all His creatures. Having had Duffy as a wonderful four-legged friend for more than 17 years, I have recognized many times in which he had seen beyond my human understanding. Heaven is going to be completely breathtaking.

God created everything, and He loves everything He created. God loves every animal and every human being, and does not destroy the spirit and soul of anything. Psalm 148:5-6, the Apocrypha's Book of Wisdom, and the Book of Nehemiah tell us God has made all living creatures to remain forever.

I am so thankful that Jesus was willing to sacrifice His sinless life for me and all creation. His suffering and agony was incredibly intense. It amazes me to realize that He did this while taking upon Himself all my sins, just so I could be adopted into God's family. Furthermore, I thank Jesus for giving His life so all the lesser creatures could be reunited with their Creator.

It is such a privilege to have dominion over creation. But that privilege entails a responsibility. It means we have been made accountable for the creatures God has put in our care. God did not give us authority over His creation so we could abuse it. God's lesser creatures are to always be treated humanely by us. Dominion does not mean domination. Domination destroys marriages, separates parents and children, corrupts companies and governments, and brings death and destruction to God's creation. God's charge of dominion is best explained in the Books of Wisdom and Proverbs.

> *God of our ancestors, Lord of mercy, who by your word have made the universe, and in your wisdom have fitted human beings to rule the creatures that you have made, to govern the world in holiness and saving justice and in honesty of soul to dispense fair judgement* (Wisdom 9:1-3 NJB).

> *A righteous man has regard for the life of his beast, but the mercy of the wicked is cruel* (Proverbs 12:10 RSV).

A proper respect for animals is seen in the Native Americans' custom of thanking God for an animal before killing it, and asking the animal to forgive them for physically destroying it. We can learn so much from our Indian neighbors.

God has a plan for His creation. As the Book of Romans indicates, life is futile without salvation. God gave man the free gift of eternal life, filled with joy and peace, just for the asking. All we have to do is reach out our hands and ask Jesus to come into our lives. In doing this, we receive the most beautiful and precious gift there is.

One day I had the opportunity to experience, to a small extent, how God must feel when He looks upon on all lost sheep (humanity) wandering around frightened, alone, and confused. It happened when I found a lost, stranded little puppy surrounded by danger.

Puppy in Crisis

It was a nice sunny day and I was driving from northern Missouri back home to St. Louis. I had been driving about four hours when I happened to look over in the grassy medium of Interstate Highway 70 and spotted a little puppy hopelessly trapped by great volumes of traffic on both sides. I knew I had to stop to save it, if possible. I slowed the car down, pulled over on the right shoulder of the highway, and backed up to get as close as possible. I got out, and the pup noticed me. I could only hope it would stay in the grassy medium until I could rescue it. I was afraid it would try to get to me and run onto the highway when I got close to it, but I had to take the chance. It seemed like an eternity passed while I waited for traffic to clear enough for me to reach the medium. I stayed quite a distance from the pup because I knew it had to trust me before I could make any type of advances to it. I knew that when you are trying to save an animal, the best thing to do is to remain as low to the ground as possible so your presence does not threaten it. I laid down in the grass and started to talk in a very low, comforting tone of voice, "Come here." I also prayed, "Dear God, please protect this little puppy and let it trust me."

I know that animals, like men, have to trust the one who is trying to help before they can become willing to put their lives in their hands. I began to realize that God cannot come to us any more than I could have gone to that little puppy. God has to wait until we trust Him and go to Him. I then knew I had to wait for the little puppy. It was very hurtful to keep waiting, not knowing if it would ever come to me, and worrying whether it would run out into traffic, but there was nothing else I could have done.

From time to time I attempted to move a little closer to the puppy, staying as low to the ground as possible, but I knew I had to wait for it to come to me. Finally, after about half an hour, it did cautiously approach me. I slowly offered my hand to be sniffed and inspected for approval, then firmly took hold of the puppy as soon as I knew it could not escape. When traffic had cleared, I carried the puppy across the highway and I put it into the rear seat of my car.

The next step was to take it home, but I had to find its family. It was noticeably well-fed, so there was no doubt that it belonged to someone, but we were out in the middle of the country, and the farmhouses were few and far between. Off we went, over winding back roads. Each time I stopped to knock on farmhouse doors, I watched to see the pup's reaction. After about another hour and a half of driving around, I discovered a farmhouse that was hidden from view, but not too far from where I had found the pup. We pulled into the driveway and the pup's tail started wagging as it paced around in the rear seat. It jumped over to the front seat, giving me puppy kisses galore. I thought that this must be the right house, but no one was home, so I could not be sure.

By then it was about 5:00 in the afternoon. I thought someone would surely be home soon, so we sat there waiting for the owners of the house to return. Fifteen minutes later, a pick-up truck arrived and out jumped a father and two little children. I opened the door of the car and before I could ask the question, "Is this your dog?" the answer was written all over the faces of both the puppy and the children. I told the father where I had found the pup and asked that he keep it fenced in, as they had a very big fenced-in yard. He said he usually does, but that the gate had been left open by accident.

To have saved the life of the little animal and to see its homecoming was a wonderful, joyful experience for me. The sacrifice of time I spent in saving and returning the little dog to its home allowed me to experience a touch of Heaven that day.

This "Puppy in Crisis" experience made me realize that Jesus wants to save us just as I had wanted to save the little puppy. I didn't know the puppy, but I knew that I wanted to save its life because I love all animals. It doesn't matter how loving or unloving they may be. I know some are afraid to show love because they are afraid they will be hurt. They don't know whom to trust, nor in whom to put their faith. We have to keep showing love, keep reaching out to them, never giving up. Even dogs that kill have most often been victimized or trained to kill. They are the ones it is really tough to communicate trust to, much like man.

Animals are in tune and at peace with nature, with God. They flow with life and death as part of their entire existence. It is man who does not understand the natural plan of God's creation. It is we who try to resist nature, to resist death and its true meaning. We live in a state of fear. Man does not understand the word *spirit*. We cannot explain how our spirit exists beyond the physical world, or even how it exists in relationship with our physical bodies. Animals are so content with it all. Their unbroken link with our Creator seems to bring them insight beyond man's mortal comprehension.

The angels were not given permission to rule the earth. That privilege and responsibility was given to man. The angels were with God before the creation of this world. They were created to fulfill the purpose for which God created them. Angels have the ability to make choices just as man does, but they do not have the right. Satan decided to be his own god, was thrown out of Heaven, and became an angel fallen from grace by his own acts. When Satan fell from grace, God took back his privileged position and Satan was without a home. He could tempt, but he could not harm; thus he was not giving man any problem. Man gave Satan his power by accepting temptation and rejecting God. Man ordered his own destruction and that of the entire physical creation—a finite world ruled by guilt, fear, anger, and death.

God could not allow sin to control His world. So God removed man from an eternal existence in this sinful state. Thus, man was given limited time on the earth. Man and all creation had to go from a non-temporal to the temporal existence spoken of in Genesis 3:19. This affected man for all eternity. It did not affect the remainder of God's creation in the same spiritual way, but it did affect their physical existence, and so affected how their soul had to deal with the temporal state in which they must live. Still, animals remained connected with God, allowing them to see beyond the temporal state.

God loves us no matter what we do. There is no sin that God cannot forgive and forget. Many people see how God's love and forgiveness can be reflected through our pets—the lovable feline, the sad-eyed horse, and other wonderful creatures. Love, loyalty, protection, companionship, respect, compassion, and sacrifice are all attributes of God. For me, those attributes also are reflected in one form of the animal kingdom known as man's best friend. How much deeper is the love of God for us?

I pray that, in our journey through the Scriptures, you will now have peace, understanding, and assurance regarding what lies ahead for the animal kingdom. I also hope you have discovered joy and peace about your own eternal destination.

I look forward to seeing Fido in Heaven, along with Duffy and Tipsy, and all the other animals I love. A more important question is this: *"Will Fido see you in Heaven?"* I don't think you will want to miss out on an eternity filled with unending wonders. It's the trip of a lifetime. It's an eternal adventure filled with joy, love, and peace. The best part of all is that it's free. Jesus has already paid for your eternal stay. All you have to do is pick up your ticket. You will find it in the Bible. Read John 3:16:

> *For God so loved the world, that he gave his only begotten Son, that whosoever believeth in him should not perish, but have everlasting life* (John 3:16 KJV).

> *That if thou shalt confess with thy mouth the Lord Jesus, and shalt believe in thine heart that God hath raised him from the dead, thou shalt be saved* (Romans 10:9 KJV).

Many Scriptures give me peace concerning the future of my pets in Heaven, Scriptures such as Romans 8:19-23; Colossians 1:15-20; Second Corinthians 5:18-19; Philippians 3:21; Psalms 96:10-13; 98:7-9; 103:22; 145:9-10,13; 148:5-6; Nehemiah 9:6; First Chronicles 16:30-34; Revelation 4:11; 5:13; Job 5:23; as well as others. I am so grateful I have the faith and assurance through the Scriptures that I will be reunited with all my pets in Heaven. My grief over losing my beloved Duffy would have been overwhelming without God's promise of the future. Duffy's passing has proven to me the strength and comfort I have in God's promise. Though there is sadness, there is also peace for now and expectation of the future reunion. I envision him now with my parents, other family members, friends, and my childhood pets. I do not doubt that they are sharing eternal bliss with the Creator.

God bless. We'll see you in Heaven.

Love,
Mary and friends

End Notes

1. *The NIV Matthew Henry Commentary*, (Grand Rapids, Michigan: Zondervan Publishing House, 1992).

2. Richard Bauckham quoted in Leon Morris' *The Cross of Jesus*, (Grand Rapids, Michigan: Wm. B. Eerdmans Publishing Company, 1988), p. 28.

3. Leon Morris, *The Cross of Jesus*, (Grand Rapids, Michigan: Wm. B. Eerdmans Publishing Company, 1988), pp. 27-28. Used with permission.

4. *Matthew Henry's Commentary*, (Harper Collins Publishing, LTD. [Grand Rapids, Michigan: Zondervan Publishing House] 1961).

5. From "The General Deliverance" in *Sermons on Several Occasions*, vol. II, (Longdon, Wesley Conference Office, 1974), pp. 281-86.

6. "A Child Blessed," in *Jesus Loved Them* by Omar Garrison, (Los Angeles, California: Ralston/Pilot, 1957).

7. George Mac Donald, *The Hope of the Gospel*, (New York: D. Appleton and Company, 1892), pp. 208, 213, 215, 223.

8. W.C. Sanderson, ed., The King James Authorized Version, (Philadelphia, Pennsylvania: A.J. Holman, 1953), pp. 18-19.

9. Dr. Elijah D. Buckner, *The Immortality of Animals*, (Philadelphia, Pennsylvania: George W. Jacoby & Co., 1903), pp. 8, 13, 34-38, 102-104, 108-109.

10.   Reverend Dr. E.F. Bush, as quoted in Dr. Buckner's *The Immortality of Animals,* pp. 37,38.

11.   Dr. Buckner, *The Immortality of Animals,* p. 38.

12.   Bishop Joseph Butler, *The Analogy of Religion: Natural and Revealed to the Constitution and Course of Nature,* (London: George Routledge and Sons, 3rd ed., 1887), pp. 12,21.

13.   Dr. Buckner, *The Immortality of Animals,* p. 60.

14.   Mary Jo Goellner, Staff writer, "Puppy Love," Suburaban Journal Newspapers of Greater St. Louis, St. Louis. Reprinted by permission.

15.   *Matthew Henry's Commentary* on Job 38:39-41.

16.   Richard Bauckham, *The Theology of the Book of Revelations,* (Cambridge University Press, 1993), pp. 33-60.

17.   Lewis B. Smedes, personal conversation, June 20, 1995.

18.   *Matthew Henry's Commentary* on Isaiah 11:6-9.

19.   *Webster's Ninth New Collegiate Dictionary,* (Springfield, Massachusetts: Merriam-Webster, Inc., 1988). All capitalizations of dog breeds follow the standards of this dictionary.

20.   Robert Eisenman and Michael Wise, *The Dead Sea Scrolls Uncovered,* (Barnes and Noble, 1994), p. 14.

Glossary

Will I See Fido in Heaven? is written to testify that animals do have eternal life. To accomplish this purpose, I realize that I must be very clear about man's relationship to eternal life. The following terms are used frequently throughout the book. The definitions provided below will help create a common understanding. They tie together the redemption of mankind with the renewing of the animals for eternal life with God.

Adoption
All those who accept Jesus as Lord become children of God. They are adopted into God's family and become joint heirs with His Son, Christ.

Beasts
A living creature, an animal. *Vine's Expository Dictionary* primarily denotes a living being (zoo, life). The English "animal" is the equivalent, stressing the fact of life as the characteristic feature. Jude 10b (KJV): "But what they know naturally, as brute beasts, in those things they corrupt themselves." A comparison to (like as that of unreasoning animals).

Blemish

I Peter 1:19 "without blemish" an, aj 299 *Amomos*, used as a technical word to designate the absence of anything amiss in a sacrifice or anything that would render it unworthy to be offered. I Peter 1:19 "without spot" an, aj 784 *Aspilos* without spot, free from spot. In I Peter 1:19 the *Amomos* (299) indicates the absence of internal blemish, and *Aspilos* that of external spot. *Vine's Expository Dictionary*: unspotted, unstained is used of a lamb (I Peter 1:19). Random House College Dictionary (1982): spotless means pure, undefiled. Scholastic Dictionary of American English (1966): immaculate means spotless. Webster's Dictionary (1939): without blemish, pure, undefiled.

Children of God

Sons and daughters of God, God's redeemed, the firstfruits of the Spirit, saints, born-again believers. All these terms refer to those in the New Testament who have accepted Jesus as their Lord and Savior, and to all those who believed in advance (in the Old Testament) for the coming Messiah.

Corruption

Physical suffering and death due to sin on all creation because of man's sins.

Creature

nn 2937 *Ktisis*-noun; *Vine's Expository Dictionary* also signifies the product of the creative act, the creature, as in Romans 1:25; 8:19. Can refer to all creatures or specific ones: man, animal, on occasion to angels. That which is created. In the New Testament, created thing (I Timothy 4:4; James 1:18; Revelation 5:3; 8:9). Creation in a passive sense, what is created, the sum total of what is created. Denotes particularly the individual creature, or what is created (Romans 1:25; 8:39; Colossians 1:15; Hebrews 4:13), the creation, all creatures.

Dominion

To rule over, to be caretakers of, to be accountable for.

Firstfruits

pr/an,nn 536—A *parche*—the first of the ripe fruits, firstfruits is always in the singular; to believers in general consecrated to God from among the rest of mankind (James 1:18; Revelation 14:4). *Vine's Expository Dictionary*: the term is applied in things spiritual, (d) to the believers of this age in relation to the <u>whole of the redeemed</u>, (II Thessalonians 2:13; James 1:18; Revelation 14:4). Notes: In James 1:18 the qualifying phrase, "a kind of," may suggest a certain falling short, on the part of those mentioned, of what they might be. In the New Berkeley Version, (Billy Graham Evangelistic Association, 1994), "all nature suffered because of man's original sin. Thus creation, as well as the creature, looks forward to deliverance from the bondage of sin" (Romans 8:19).

Grace	The unmerited favor of God. (See Ephesians 1:3-8 KJV and II Corinthians 5:17-21 KJV).
Living Being	Most often refers to all living creatures/living souls.
Non-temporal Realm	The eternal, timeless plane in which the spirit relates. It is the immortal existence.
Perish	*Vine's Greek Dictionary* says, "to corrupt, to spoil or figuratively to deprave, to destroy, being brought into an inferior or worst condition, a destruction or corruption, ethically, with a moral significance—of the effect upon themselves." Referring to the word *perish* in Matthew 8:25, *Vine's Greek Dictionary* says "to destroy."
Reconciliation	To settle differences with others. To be in harmony again.
Redeemed	All the children of God who have been taught to accept Jesus Christ as their Lord and Savior have been acquitted of their sins.
Sacrifices in the Old Testament for Sin	An animal's blood had to be shed to cover man's sins in order that the sinner might be forgiven, yet the blood of the animal could not itself take away sins. It did allow the sinner to see that God, in forgiving sins, was not ignoring those sins, but dealing with them. Thus, God was able to pass over the sins of believers of former generations temporarily. In a sense, He forgave on credit

	as people looked ahead for the coming Messiah.
Sinless	Righteous, innocent, spotless, pure, redeemed, upright.
Temporal Plane	The environment as it pertains to time. It is our mortal existence. The body and soul can only relate to the temporal plane. It refers to the physical/psychological world in which we live.
Vanity	(Romans 8:20), *Mataiotes*—inutility; moral depravity. *Lexical Aids*: vanity, nothingness, worthlessness; used in Romans 8:20 to show the emptiness of the present in contrast with the living fullness of the future (Ephesians 4:17; II Peter 2:18). *Vine's Expository Dictionary*: emptiness as to results akin to *Mataiotes* (see empty, vain) is used of the creation (Romans 8:20), as failing of the results designed, owing to sin.
Works	Can mean all of God's creation (plants, animals, sun, rocks, etc.). It can be works to gain God's favor or miracles of God, His actions, transactions, or activities.

Additional Suggested Reading

The Cross of Jesus by Leon Morris, (Wm. B. Eerdmans Publishing Co., Grand Rapids, Michigan).

Angels on Assignment by Charles and Frances Hunter, (Hunter Books, Kingwood, Texas).

I Saw Heaven by Roberts Liardon, (Harrison House, Tulsa, Oklahoma).

The Theology of the Book of Revelation by Richard Bauckham, (Cambridge University Press, England).

Forgive & Forget–Healing the Hurts We Don't Deserve by Lewis B. Smedes, (Pocket Books, a division of Simon & Schuster, Inc.).

Biblical Publication Information

Holy Bible Authorized King James Version (KJV), The Holy Bible Self-pronouncing King James Authorized Version of the Holy Bible, Containing the Old and New Testaments, Translated out of the Original Tongues; and with the Former Translations Diligently Compared and Revised; with Self-pronouncing Reference Dictionary Index, published by A. J. Holman in Philadelphia in 1937, and revised and edited by W. C. Sanderson.

Holy Bible Unauthorized King James Version (KJV), (1943).

New American Bible with Revised New Testament (NAB), (The Confraternity of Christian Doctrine, Inc., 1986.

New Catholic Edition of the Holy Bible, (1948).

Revised Standard Version of the Bible (RSV), (The Division of Christian Education of the National Council of Churches of Christ in the USA, 1946, 1952).

The Amplified Bible (AMP), (Grand Rapids, Michigan: Zondervan Bible Publishers, 1965).

The Bible in Today's English Version (The Good News Bible) (TEV), (American Bible Society 1966, 1971, 1976, 1992).

The Holy Bible, The Student Bible New International Version (NIV), (Zondervan Bible Publishers, 1973, 1978, 1984.

The International Inductive Study New Testament, (New Berkeley Version), (Billy Graham Evangelistic Association, 1994).

The Living Bible paraphrased (TLB), (Tyndale House Publishers, Inc., 1971). Used by permission. All rights reserved.

The New Jerusalem Bible (NJB), (Darton, Longman & Todd, Ltd. And Doubleday, a division of Bantam Doubleday Dell Publishing Group, Inc., 1985). Used by permission.

Douay-Rheims Bible, Old Testament 1609, New Testament 1582. Printed by Tan Books and Publishers, Inc., Rockford, Illinois 61105, 1899.

The Holy Scriptures, The Jewish Publication Society of America, 1917.

The Dead Sea Scrolls Uncovered, © Element Books Limited 1992 Text © Robert Eisenman and Michael Wise 1992 1994 Barnes & Noble Books

About the Author

Mary Buddemeyer-Porter is an author, educator, lecturer, television producer and Regional EMMY-nominated songwriter. She also is creator of the "Land of Music" music education series and President of Note Family, Inc.

Mary was born on a small farm in northwest Missouri and was raised in a wonderful Christian family with her brother, Mac Allen. Today she is a wife with two grown sons, six grand-children, and four dogs.

Mary has spent the better part of her life studying the Bible, with special concentration on the Biblical perspective of the immortality of animals since 1990.

If you have any animal stories to share, please call 636-227-3078 or write:

EDEN Publications
P.O. Box 789
Manchester, MO 63011
www.creaturesinheaven.com